Practical Introduction to ISO 27001

Based On the Latest Version Of ISO/IEC 27001:2022 Requirements And Its 2024 Amendment

Ben Pournader
Behzad Saei

Practical Introduction to ISO 27001

Based on the latest version of ISO/IEC 27001:2022 and its 2024 amendment

By *Ben Pournader, and Behzad Saei*
August 2024, U.S.A.

Every possible effort has been made to ensure that the information contained in this book is accurate at the time of writing. However, the authors cannot accept any responsibility for any errors or omissions. There is no responsibility for loss or damage to any person or organization acting, or refraining from action, as a result of material in this book.

ISBN: 9798336206838

Contents

Who Should Read This Book?

This book is designed for security professionals who aim to implement and manage security frameworks and controls within their organizations. It is ideal for security managers, IT consultants, IT auditors, management professionals, and anyone aspiring to work in the field of information security. Even beginners seeking to learn about information security concepts can benefit from this book, as it requires only a basic understanding of security concepts and does not demand expertise with security tools.

The book is written for all stakeholders involved in an organization's Information Security Program, including IT managers, information security engineers, IT systems and network administrators, software application developers, database administrators, legal and compliance team members, and occasionally, individuals in finance, marketing, sales, and HR departments.

Whether you work in a large organization with a dedicated information security department or a small business with limited personnel and security tools, this book is for you. It provides valuable insights into ISO 27001 concepts and the management of an information security program.

We believe this book serves as both a simple, easy-to-read introduction to ISO 27001 and a deeper dive into some of its requirements. Organized to accommodate beginners with no prior security experience, it offers clear insights into the ISO 27001 audit cycle. Each chapter is purposeful, but you can choose to skip chapters and focus on the ones that meet your needs. For example, if you are an experienced security professional, you might skip the chapter titled "What is Information Security." However, for the best results, we recommend reading all the chapters sequentially.

What is Information Security?

Information security is nothing but activities and measures to protect both information and information systems from unauthorized access, use, disclosure, disruption, modification, or destruction. We can also say information security is implementing administrative, technical, and finally physical safeguards to ensure the confidentiality, integrity, and availability of information and information systems to a certain level. This can include measures such as encryption, firewalls, antivirus technologies, access control lists, security policies, security awareness training and much more.

The goal of information security is to protect information systems and sensitive information by preventing unauthorized people from gaining access to them, which can have serious consequences, such as financial loss, reputational damage to the organizations, and loss of privacy of customers or employees.

Why ISO 27001?

ISO 27001:2022 is an international standard for information security, cybersecurity and privacy protection that outlines the requirements for an Information Security Management System (ISMS). Obtaining a certification for ISO 27001 provides lots of benefits including:

1. Improved information security: Implementing an ISMS that meets the requirements of ISO 27001 can help organizations to improve the security of their information and information assets and reduce the risk of data breaches by practicing information protection and mitigating information risks. This includes protecting information from unauthorized access, use, disclosure, disruption, modification, or destruction.

2. Enhanced reputation and credibility: Obtaining ISO 27001 certification demonstrates to customers, partners, suppliers, and other stakeholders that the organization takes information security seriously, and it is capable of protecting sensitive information. This can enhance the reputation and credibility of the organization.

3. Competitive advantage: ISO 27001 certification can provide organizations with a competitive advantage over non-certified organizations, as it demonstrates a commitment to information security, which can be attractive to customers and other stakeholders.

4. Compliance with regulations: ISO 27001 certification in some cases can help organizations to comply with various regulations. As an example, the Committee on Foreign Investment in the United States (CFIUS) may require a company to align with ISO 27001 and/or NIST 800-171 standard.

5. Continual improvement: ISO 27001 certification requires reviews and annual internal and external audits, which can help organizations to identify opportunities for improvement and ensure that their ISMS remains effective.

6. Complying with contract obligations: Contractual obligation refers to the legal and binding responsibilities and duties that parties agree to fulfill as a part of a contract. As an example, a customer can ask a service provider to show that they are compliant with a certain security standard or regulation or show that they are compliant with ISO 27001.

What Distinguishes ISO 27001 from Other Security Frameworks?

ISO 27001 is one of many information security standards and frameworks, each with its own focus, structure, and intended use.

Scope

ISO 27001 covers all aspects of an organization's Information Security Management System (ISMS), making it a comprehensive standard. While other frameworks like PCI DSS or HIPAA focus on specific areas, ISO 27001 encompasses the entire ISMS, ensuring a broad and inclusive approach to information security.

Holistic Approach

ISO 27001 offers a complete ISMS that can be applied to any organization, regardless of its industry. This holistic approach contrasts with other standards like PCI DSS and HIPAA, which have more limited scopes tailored to specific sectors (payment card industry and healthcare, respectively). This makes ISO 27001 versatile and applicable across various industries.

Industry-Agnostic

ISO 27001 is not tied to any specific industry, allowing it to be utilized by any organization. In contrast, many other security standards are industry-specific, limiting their applicability. This industry-agnostic nature of ISO 27001 makes it a flexible and universally applicable standard for managing information security.

Risk Analysis

One of the core components of ISO 27001 is its focus on risk analysis. The standard helps organizations identify, analyze, and manage information security risks through a continuous cycle of improvement. This proactive risk management approach ensures that organizations can better handle potential security threats and comply with various industry standards.

Certification

Achieving ISO 27001 certification can be more expensive than other frameworks due to the requirement of hiring a third-party auditor. Additionally, ISO 27001 certification is only valid for three years, necessitating periodic reassessment and re-certification, which adds to the overall cost.

Internal Audit

ISO 27001 places significant emphasis on internal audits to ensure that the ISMS is functioning correctly and continuously improving. Regular internal audits help organizations identify areas of non-compliance and take corrective actions promptly, maintaining the integrity of the ISMS.

Continual Improvement

Continual improvement is a fundamental principle of ISO 27001. The standard encourages organizations to constantly evaluate and enhance their ISMS to adapt to evolving security threats and changes in the organizational environment. This focus on continual improvement ensures that the ISMS remains effective and up-to-date.

Emphasis on Documentation

ISO 27001 requires comprehensive documentation to support the implementation and maintenance of the ISMS. Detailed documentation provides a clear and structured approach to managing information security, ensuring transparency, accountability, and consistency across the organization.

Management Support for Implementation

Successful implementation of ISO 27001 requires strong support from top management. The standard emphasizes the importance of management commitment to ensure adequate resources, support, and leadership are provided for the ISMS. This top-down approach is crucial for fostering a security-aware culture within the organization and ensuring the effective implementation of information security practices.

Why is ISO 27001 so Popular?

ISO 27001, the international standard for information security management systems (ISMS), has gained widespread popularity for several compelling reasons. ISO 27001's popularity stems from its universal applicability, simplicity, alignment with other management systems, time-tested principles, abundant resources, certification opportunities, influence on other standards, and its role in fostering a common language among information security professionals. These factors collectively contribute to its status as a leading standard for information security management.

1. Universal Applicability: ISO 27001 is designed to be applicable to all types of organizations, regardless of their size, industry, or nature. This universal applicability makes it a versatile standard that can be adopted by small businesses, large enterprises, non-profits, and governmental entities alike, ensuring a

broad relevance across different sectors.

2. Simplicity and Brevity: The standard itself is concise, spanning just 20 pages. Its simplicity lies in its core structure, which revolves around an ISMS and a set of information security controls. This straightforward approach makes it easier for organizations to understand and implement, without being overwhelmed by complexity.

3. Alignment with Other Management Systems: ISO 27001 is aligned with other widely recognized management systems, such as Quality Management Systems (QMS), Privacy Information Management Systems (PIMS), Service Management Systems (SMS), and Business Continuity Management Systems (BCMS). This alignment facilitates integration and streamlines processes for organizations that already adhere to other ISO standards.

4. Time-Tested Framework: The origins of ISO 27001 date back to 1995 with the publication of BS 7799-1. Over the years, the standard has evolved and been refined, benefiting from decades of practical application and feedback. This long-standing history has contributed to its robustness and reliability.

5. Simple but Valuable Principles: ISO 27001 is built on fundamental principles that are both straightforward and highly effective. These include understanding the needs and expectations of interested parties, demonstrating leadership and commitment, maintaining proper documentation, pursuing continual improvement, adopting a process approach, and applying a risk-based approach. These principles provide a solid foundation for a comprehensive information security strategy and robust information security program.

6. Abundant Resources and Support: A wealth of additional recommendations, guidelines, and training courses are available for ISO 27001. This extensive support network makes it easier for organizations to implement and maintain the standard, ensuring they have access to the latest best practices and expert

advice.

7. Certification Opportunities: Organizations can choose to certify their ISMS against ISO 27001, which can be a significant advantage in certain industries and countries where certification is a mandatory requirement. Certification demonstrates a commitment to information security and provides assurance to customers, partners, and regulators.

8. Influence on Other Standards: Many other information security standards and frameworks draw inspiration from ISO 27001. Its principles and structure have influenced the development of various other guidelines, making it a cornerstone of information security practices globally.

9. Common Language Among Professionals: ISO 27001 is widely used by information security professionals, creating a common language and understanding within the industry. This shared framework facilitates communication, collaboration, and knowledge exchange among professionals, enhancing the overall effectiveness of information security efforts.

What Is an ISMS?

An Information Security Management System (ISMS) is simply an information security program with a comprehensive approach to manage an organization's information security activities, tools, resources, budget, processes and policies. It is a systematic framework and ongoing process that includes planning, creating, maintaining, implementing, and monitoring information security policies, procedures, and technologies to protect information assets from unauthorized access, use, disclosure, disruption, modification, or destruction.

By using ISO 27xxx family of standards, an organization has the ability to design, develop, implement and maintain an ISMS which is nothing but a structured framework to manage the security of their information systems and information assets, including but not limited to intellectual property, financial information, employee information, and/or information passed to them by their customers or third parties.

An Information Security Management System (ISMS) may include the following essential items:

1. Scope

Defining the boundaries and applicability of the information security management system is required to establish the scope. The consideration in determining the scope includes the external and internal issues as well as the interfaces and dependencies between activities performed by the organization, and those that are performed by other organizations. The ISO 27001 scope statement may cover what your organization does, what important information is covered by the ISMS and why security is important for your organization and finally, which parts of your organization are to be certified.
Bear in mind that the scope of an ISMS must be documented per ISO 27001.

Here are some examples of ISO/IEC 27001 scope statements:

1. **Example 1: IT Services Company**
   - ○ Scope: "The ISMS covers all information assets, processes, and services managed by the IT department, including data centers, cloud services, network infrastructure, and support services at the headquarters located in San Francisco, CA. and two other locations for data centers: San Jose, CA and Las Vegas, NV."

2. **Example 2: Financial Institution (Bank)**
   - ○ Scope: "The ISMS applies to the management of customer financial data, transaction processing systems, and associated support functions within the bank's main office and regional branches in North America."

3. **Example 3: Healthcare Provider**
   - ○ Scope: "The ISMS encompasses all patient information management systems, electronic health records (EHR), and related support services at the main hospital and all affiliated clinics within the state of Texas.

4. **Example 4: Manufacturing Company**
   - ○ Scope: "The ISMS includes all production control systems, supply chain management processes, and associated IT infrastructure at the main manufacturing facility and distribution center in Detroit, MI."

5. **Example 5: E-commerce Business**
   - ○ Scope: "The ISMS covers the protection of customer data, payment processing systems, and e-commerce platform operations managed from the company's headquarters and data centers in New York, NY."

6. **Example 6: Government Agency**
   - ○ Scope: "The ISMS applies to the management of confidential government records, communication systems, and support services within the agency's central office and all regional offices across the country."

These examples demonstrate how the scope of ISO 27001 can vary depending on the nature of the organization, its products, its processes, and/or the specific information assets that need protection. As you see in the above example, the scope is clearly defined to ensure that all relevant aspects of the organization's ISMS are covered and adequately protected.

2. Asset Management

Asset management enables organizations to realize value from their assets in line with their objectives while balancing financial, environmental, and social factors. The benefits of effective asset management include:

- Improved Financial Performance: Enhanced asset utilization and cost management contribute to better financial results.
- Informed Investment Decisions: Data-driven insights enable more strategic and effective capital investments.
- Risk Management: Proactive identification and mitigation of risks ensure stability and security.
- Enhanced Services: Improved asset performance leads to higher quality and more reliable services.
- Social Responsibility: Demonstrating commitment to ethical and sustainable practices enhances social value.
- Regulatory Compliance: Adhering to relevant standards and regulations prevents legal issues and penalties.
- Reputation Enhancement: A strong asset management strategy builds trust and confidence among stakeholders.
- Sustainability Improvement: Efficient resource use and long-term planning support environmental sustainability.
- Increased Efficiency and Effectiveness: Streamlined processes and optimized asset use drive productivity.

Understanding Assets

An asset is anything valuable to an organization, with varying value for different organizations and stakeholders. The value of an asset can change over time and may extend beyond one organization's responsibility. Assets can be grouped based on type, system, or portfolio to leverage added benefits.

Strategic Management of Assets

Organizations should implement planning, control activities, and monitoring to exploit opportunities and mitigate risks to an acceptable level. Asset management involves balancing costs, opportunities, and risks to achieve organizational objectives across different timeframes. It allows for the examination of asset needs and performance at various levels and the application of analytical approaches throughout the asset's life cycle, including potential post-disposal liabilities.

Core Fundamentals of Asset Management

1. Value: Assets exist to provide value to the organization and its stakeholders. The value is determined by the organization's objectives, and asset management aligns with these objectives through clear statements and comprehensive life cycle management.
2. Alignment: Asset management translates organizational objectives into technical and financial decisions, plans, and activities. It integrates with functional processes and implements a supporting asset management system to ensure coherence and coordination.
3. Leadership: Successful asset management relies on strong leadership and a supportive workplace culture. Clearly defined roles, competent employees, and active stakeholder consultation are essential for driving asset management initiatives forward.
4. Assurance: Asset management ensures that assets fulfill their intended purpose through robust processes for capability assessment, monitoring, and continual

improvement. This is supported by the necessary resources and skilled personnel.

ISO 55001:2024, Asset management — Asset management system — Requirements, is a good reference to be considered for implementation of a robust Asset Management Program.

3. Risk Assessment

Risk management is needed in order to make risk-aware decisions. It involves identifying, evaluating, and prioritizing potential security risks and/or threats, and choosing an appropriate response to mitigate, avoid or transfer the identified risk. Accepting the risk is another response option if we conclude that the risk score is low, i.e. the impact and/or the likelihood of that threat is less than a certain amount.

Companies aiming to enhance their risk management processes can consider conforming to ISO 31000. ISO 31000 is an international standard that provides principles and guidelines for effective risk management. Adopting ISO 31000 helps organizations identify, assess, and mitigate risks systematically and consistently but you can use any risk management process for your ISMS.

4. Security Policies & Procedures

Documented policies and procedures serve as the foundation for your organization's information security strategy. They articulate the methods and measures your organization employs to achieve and maintain a certain level of information security. These documents provide clear guidelines on acceptable behavior and the proper use of information systems, ensuring that all employees understand their roles and responsibilities in protecting organizational assets.

5. Access Control Management

Access control management involves overseeing who is granted access to specific information and information systems within an organization. It encompasses the processes for provisioning, reviewing, modifying, revoking, and generally regulating access to ensure that only authorized individuals can access sensitive data and systems.

6. Training and Awareness

Security awareness training is about educating stakeholders like data owners, system owners, employees, and contractors about the importance of information security and best methods to protect both information and information systems.

7. Incident Response

The time is gone when organizations focused on just preventing security incidents. Nowadays they clearly understand that security incidents are inevitable, and nobody is hack-proof. So, in addition to implementing prevention mechanisms, they have corrective mechanisms in place to recover quickly from the unavoidable incidents that were mentioned above.

Incident response processes need a documented plan called Incident Response Plan (IRP) to respond to security incidents. It should cover procedures to identify, evaluate, report, and manage incidents. The main purpose of an Incident Response Plan is to minimize the impact of security incidents on the business and restore normal business operations as quickly as possible. It is also beneficial to prevent similar incidents from reoccurring in the future.

8. Implementing Technical Tools

Implementing security tools is an essential component of any effective information security program. It helps organizations to protect sensitive information, detect and respond to security incidents, improve their overall security posture, and automate security processes.

9. Continuous Monitoring & Improvement

Continuous monitoring and re-assessment involve regularly evaluating the effectiveness of the Information Security Management System (ISMS) and making improvements as needed. One of the essential tools for continuous monitoring is the use of key performance indicators (KPIs). KPIs are specific, measurable metrics used to evaluate the effectiveness of the ISMS. They provide quantitative data that helps in assessing the performance of various security aspects.

These are some examples of Security KPIs that you can use to monitor your ISMS performance:

- **Incident Response Time**: Measures the time taken to detect, respond to, and mitigate security incidents.
- **Number of Security Incidents**: Tracks the frequency of security breaches, attempted attacks, and vulnerabilities detected over a period.
- **User Compliance Rates**: Monitors the adherence of employees to security policies and procedures, such as password management or data handling practices.
- **Patch Management Efficiency**: Evaluates the speed and effectiveness of applying security patches and updates to systems and software.
- **System Uptime and Availability**: Ensures that critical systems and applications are available and functioning without interruptions.

Benefits of Implementing ISMS

Implementing an Information Security Management System (ISMS) based on ISO 27001 offers a multitude of benefits for organizations including improved security and resilience, enhanced awareness and culture, risk reduction, increased stakeholder trust, compliance, process maturity, budget transparency, and marketing advantages. These benefits collectively contribute to a stronger, more secure, and more competitive organization.

1. Improved Overall Security Posture and Cyber Resilience: ISO 27001 provides a systematic approach to managing sensitive company information, ensuring that risks are identified and mitigated. This leads to a stronger security posture and enhances the organization's resilience against cyber threats and attacks.

2. Raising Awareness and Information Security Culture: Implementing ISO 27001 involves training and educating employees about information security policies and practices. This helps foster a culture of security awareness throughout the organization, where everyone understands their role in protecting information assets.

3. Reducing Cybersecurity and Business Risks: By identifying and addressing vulnerabilities, ISO 27001 helps reduce the likelihood and impact of cybersecurity incidents. Additionally, the risk management framework extends beyond cybersecurity to encompass broader business risks, contributing to overall organizational stability.

4. Building Stakeholder Trust (External and Internal): Achieving ISO 27001 certification demonstrates a commitment to information security, which can significantly enhance trust among customers, partners, and other stakeholders. Internally, it assures employees that the organization prioritizes protecting its information assets.

5. Legal, Regulatory, and Contractual Compliance: ISO 27001 helps organizations comply with various legal,

regulatory, and contractual requirements related to information security. This reduces the risk of non-compliance penalties and enhances the organization's reputation as a trustworthy entity.

6. A Common Approach to Compliance: ISO 27001 provides a standardized framework for meeting diverse information security requirements. This common approach simplifies compliance efforts, especially for organizations operating in multiple jurisdictions or under various regulatory frameworks.

7. Increasing the Maturity of Related Processes: The implementation of ISO 27001 often leads to improvements in related processes, such as IT, human resources, and operations. By integrating information security considerations into these areas, the overall maturity and effectiveness of these processes are enhanced.

8. Increasing Transparency and Justification of Information Security Budgets: ISO 27001 requires a thorough risk assessment and management process, which provides clear insights into the organization's security needs. This transparency helps justify information security budgets and ensures that resources are allocated efficiently and effectively.

9. Marketing Opportunities: Being ISO 27001 certified can be a powerful marketing tool. It signals to potential customers and partners that the organization takes information security seriously, providing a competitive edge in the marketplace. It can also open doors to new business opportunities, especially with clients who require stringent security measures from their vendors.

ISO 27000, ISO 27001, and ISO 27002

ISO 27000, ISO 27001, and ISO 27002 are interconnected standards in the field of information security management.

ISO 27xxx is a family of more than a dozen standards that provides a comprehensive overview of information security management and includes guidelines to manage and protect sensitive information. The standards in the ISO 27xxx family cover a wide range of topics, including risk management, access control, physical security, auditing, privacy protection, incident management and much more.

ISO 27001

ISO 27001 is a specific standard within the ISO 27xxx family that outlines the requirements for an Information Security Management System (ISMS). As mentioned above, an ISMS is a systematic approach to protect information and information against unauthorized access, use, disclosure, disruption, modification, or destruction.

Like other standards in the ISO 27xxx family, ISO 27001 can be purchased from your national ISO member or through the ISO store. As an example, you can purchase the standard from https://www.iso.org or American National Standards Institute (ANSI) online store at https://webstore.ansi.org
ANSI is the US member body to ISO and, via its US National Committee, the International Electrotechnical Commission (IEC). You can also purchase some ISO 27XXX standards like the ISO 27001 standard from the Amazon website.

ISO 27000

ISO 27000 provides the overview of information security management systems (ISMS), and terms and definitions commonly used in the ISO 27xxx family of standards. In other words, ISO 27000 provides an understanding of how the different standards in the ISO 27xxx family of standards fit together, their scopes, roles, functions and relationship to each other. ISO 27000 is a very useful document for ISO 27001 implementers and auditors since it brings together all the essential terminology used by other standards in the ISO 27xxx family. ISO 27000:2018 (or we better call it ISO/IEC 27000:2018) has been developed by a joint technical committee ISO/IEC JTC 1, Information technology, subcommittee SC 27, IT security techniques, whose secretariat is held by DIN, the ISO member for Germany.

Note: *In more than 90 percent of cases when somebody talks about ISO 27000, they mean either ISO 27001 or ISO 27xxx series!*

ISO 27002

ISO 27002 is another standard in the ISO 27xxx series and is a supplementary standard that focuses on the comprehensive explanation of information security controls that are listed in Annex A of ISO 27001 standard so we can simply say that ISO 27002 provides lots of potential controls and control mechanisms that are designed to be implemented with the guidelines provided in ISO 27001 standard.

Organizations can achieve certification to ISO 27001 by demonstrating that they have implemented an ISMS that meets the requirements of the standard but there is no certification available for ISO 27000 or ISO 27002.

Standards in ISO 27xxx Family

As mentioned previously, ISO 27xxx is a family of more than a dozen inter-woven standards, already published or under development, that provides a comprehensive overview of information security management and includes guidelines to manage and protect sensitive information. The standards in the ISO 27xxx family cover a wide range of topics to either support or complement ISO 27001. Some of the most important of them are listed here:

ISO 27000

ISO 27000 is an overview and introduction to the ISO27xxx series and brings together all the essential terminology used by other standards in the ISO 27xxx family.

ISO 27001

ISO 27001 is the most important standard in this family and lists the Information Security Management System (ISMS) requirements. It is the standard that specifies a certifiable ISMS and its requirements for the implementation of information security controls customized to the needs of individual organizations. ISO 27001 can be used by all organizations, regardless of type, size and nature.

ISO 27002

ISO 27002 is a comprehensive catalog of lots of information security controls. It provides a list of common information security controls, their objectives, and best practices to be used as implementation guidance when selecting and implementing information security controls to implement an ISMS.

Conformance is the word that comes with ISO 27002. The term "conformance" is often misunderstood and sometimes confused with "compliance." The ISO 27002 code of practice provides guidance and recommendations, rather than serving as a conformance assessment standard. In the ISO technical sense, a management system standard uses "shall" statements to indicate requirements, as seen in ISO 27001. In contrast, ISO 27002 uses "should" statements, indicating recommendations rather than mandatory requirements. Therefore, it's important to ensure that claims of conformance are accurate and not misleading.

ISO 27003

ISO 27003 is a very useful and pragmatic guidance on how to implement an ISMS per ISO 27001.

ISO 27004

ISO 27004 is about information security management metrics to monitor, measure, analyze and evaluate performance and the effectiveness of an ISMS. ISO 27004 addresses 1. Monitoring and measurement of information security performance, 2. Monitoring and measurement of the effectiveness of an ISMS including its processes as well as its controls, 3. Analyzing and evaluating the results of monitoring and measurement.

ISO 27005

ISO 27005 provides guidelines for information security risk management. Bear in mind that it is not required to adopt the risk management process that is explained in ISO 27005. You can use any risk management methods for implementing an ISMS.

ISO 27006-1

ISO 27006 is a guide to ISO 27001 ISMS certification. It covers the requirements and provides guidance for bodies providing audit and certification of an ISMS in accordance with ISO 27001. It is primarily intended to support the accreditation of certification bodies providing ISO 27001 certification.

ISO 27006-2

ISO 27006-2 is a guide to ISO 27701 Privacy Information Management System (PIMS) certification. It specifies requirements and provides guidance for bodies providing audit and certification of a PIMS according to ISO 27701 in combination with ISO 27001, in addition to the requirements contained in ISO 27006 and ISO 27701.

ISO 27007

ISO 27007 provides guidance on the ISMS audit program, on conducting audits, and on the competence of ISMS auditors, in addition to the guidance contained in ISO 19011. (ISO 19011 is a guideline about auditing any kind of management systems. It covers the principles of auditing and managing an audit program for auditing management systems).

ISO 27008

ISO 27008 focuses on the assessment of technical controls of an ISMS. It provides guidance on reviewing and assessing the implementation and operation of information security controls, especially the technical assessment of information system controls.

ISO 27009

ISO 27009 is a standard discussing how to change the controls of ISO 27001 or ISO 27002 or add a new control for a specified domain, application area or market. It ensures that additional or refined requirements are not in conflict with the requirements in ISO 27001

ISO 27010

ISO 27010 is about implementing information security management within information sharing communities i.e. information security management for inter-sector and inter-organizational communications.

ISO 27011

ISO 27011 is an information security management guideline based on ISO 27002 for telecommunications organizations.

ISO 27013

ISO 27013 provides guidance on integrated implementation of ISO 27001 and ISO 20000-1 for organizations intending to either implement ISO 27001 when ISO 20000-1 is already implemented (or vice versa) or implement both ISO 27001 and ISO 20000-1 at the same time. ISO 20000-1 is about implementing, maintaining and continually improving service management systems (SMS). ISO 27001 and ISO 20000-1 can also be integrated with other management system standards, like ISO 9001, ISO 14001 or ISO 45001.

ISO 27014

ISO 27014 is about concepts, objectives and processes for the governance of information security. ISO 27014 is about "governance" of an ISMS while ISO 27001 is about the "management" of it.

ISO 27016

ISO 27016 covers the economic consequences of decisions about information protection in the context of competing requirements for resources in an organization. It provides a methodology to better understand economically for the organizations on how to more accurately value their identified information assets, value the potential risks to those information assets, appreciate the value that information protection controls deliver to these information assets, and finally determine the optimum level of resources to be applied in securing these information assets.

ISO 27017

ISO 27017 is one of the popular standards these days which provides additional controls that specifically relate to cloud services and cloud computing.

ISO 27018

ISO 27018 is another popular standard that focuses on protection of personally identifiable information (PII) in public clouds acting as PII processors in accordance with the privacy principles in ISO 29100.

ISO 27019

ISO 27019 covers information security controls for the (non-nuclear) energy utility industry for controlling and monitoring the production/generation, transmission, storage, and distribution of electric power, gas, oil and heat.

ISO 27021

ISO 27021 is a standard explaining the competencies and skills which are required by infosec management professionals leading or involved in establishing, implementing, maintaining and continually improving one or more information security management system processes of an ISMS.

ISO 27022

ISO 27022 defines a Process Reference Model (PRM) for information security management.

ISO 27024

ISO 27024 is an under-development standard and is going to list some laws and regulations related to information security and the use of ISO 27xxx family of standards in governmental or regulatory requirements.

ISO 27028

ISO 27028 is an under-development standard and is going to cover guidance on the use and development of attributes aligned with ISO 27002.

ISO 27029

ISO 27029 is another under development standard and is going to offer ISO 27002 relationship with ISO and IEC standards.

ISO 27031

ISO 27031 covers the concepts of Information and Communication Technology (ICT) readiness for Business Continuity (BC). It provides a framework to identify and specify different aspects (such as performance criteria, design, and implementation) of improving an organization's ICT readiness to ensure resilience and business continuity

ISO 27032

ISO 27032 provides guidance for improving the state of cybersecurity and its dependencies on other security domains like information security, network security, internet security, and critical information infrastructure protection. Bear in mind that cybersecurity is not equal to information security. In information security, our primary concern is protecting the confidentiality, integrity, and availability of the data. In cybersecurity, the primary concern is protecting against unauthorized electronic access to the data/information.

ISO 27033

ISO 27033 standards are about IT network security. ISO 27033 specifically addresses the technical and operational aspects of securing network infrastructures and data transmission. It has 6 different documents: ISO 27033-1 to ISO 27033-6.

ISO 27034

ISO 27034 provides guidance for application security and is like ISO 27033 that has different documents: ISO 27033-1 to ISO 27033-7

ISO 27035

ISO 27035 concerns information security incident management and it is also a multi-part international standard (like ISO 27032 and ISO 27033) that provides a five-step process for managing information security incidents and outlines the processes and principles for handling information security incidents, from preparation and detection to response and recovery.

ISO 27036

ISO 27036 is another multi-part standard (it comes in 4 parts) and is about information security guidelines for ICT supply chains including cloud computing. The standard addresses the information security risks associated with supplier relationships and offers best practices for managing these kinds of risks.

ISO 27037

ISO 27037 focuses on the identification, collection, and preservation of digital evidence.

ISO 27038

ISO 27038 specifies guidelines for the redaction of digital documents.

ISO 27039

ISO 27039 offers guidance to help organizations prepare for the deployment of intrusion detection and prevention systems (IDPS). This standard covers the selection, implementation, and operation of IDPS, providing essential background information to support these guidelines.

ISO 27040

ISO 27040 outlines technical requirements and guidance for organizations to effectively mitigate risks through a consistent approach to planning, designing, documenting, and implementing data storage security. This standard addresses the protection of data both when stored in information and communications technology (ICT) systems and during transit across communication links associated with storage. It encompasses the security of storage devices and media, management activities related to these devices and media, applications and services, and the control or monitoring of user activities throughout the devices' and media's lifecycle, including post-use or end-of-life stages.

ISO 27041

ISO 27041 offers guidance on ensuring that methods and processes for investigating information security incidents are "fit for purpose." It encompasses best practices for defining requirements, describing methods, and demonstrating that implementations meet these requirements. The standard also addresses how vendor and third-party testing can contribute to this assurance process.

ISO 27042

ISO 27042 provides guidance on analyzing and interpreting digital evidence, ensuring continuity, validity, reproducibility, and repeatability. It outlines best practices for selecting, designing, and implementing analytical processes and for recording sufficient information to enable independent scrutiny. Additionally, it offers guidance on mechanisms for demonstrating the proficiency and competence of the investigation team.

ISO 27043

ISO 27043 focuses on incident investigation and eForensics, offering guidelines based on idealized models for common investigation processes across various scenarios involving digital evidence. These guidelines cover the entire process, from pre-incident preparation to investigation closure, and provide general advice and caveats. The principles and processes described are applicable to various types of investigations, including unauthorized access, data corruption, system crashes, corporate information security breaches, and other digital investigations.

ISO 27050

ISO 27050 focuses on eDiscovery and digital forensics, divided into four parts:
- ISO 27050-1: This part is relevant to both technical and non-technical personnel involved in electronic discovery activities.
- ISO 27050-2: It provides guidance for senior management, both technical and non-technical, within an organization. It includes those responsible for compliance with statutory and regulatory requirements and industry standards.
- ISO 27050-3: This part outlines requirements and recommendations for electronic discovery activities,

including identification, preservation, collection, processing, review, analysis, and production of Electronically Stored Information (ESI). It also specifies measures that cover the entire ESI lifecycle, from initial creation to final disposition.

- ISO 27050-4: This part offers guidance on planning, preparing for, and implementing electronic discovery from both technological and process perspectives. It includes proactive measures to enable effective and appropriate electronic discovery processes.

ISO 27070

ISO 27070 specifies the security requirements for establishing virtualized roots of trust in the cloud.

ISO 27071

ISO 27071 provides a framework and recommendations for establishing trusted connections between devices and services using hardware security modules. It includes guidelines for components such as hardware security modules, roots of trust, identity, authentication and key establishment, remote attestation, and data integrity and authenticity.

This standard is applicable to scenarios where trusted connections between devices and services are established based on hardware security modules.

ISO 27099

ISO 27099 establishes a framework of requirements for managing information security for Public Key Infrastructure (PKI) trust service providers through certificate policies and certificate practice statements, supported by an Information Security Management System (ISMS) where applicable. This framework includes assessing and addressing information security risks to meet users' agreed service requirements as specified through the certificate policy. It also aids trust service providers in supporting multiple certificate policies. The document covers the lifecycle of public key certificates used for digital signatures, authentication, and key establishment for data encryption. It does not cover authentication methods, non-repudiation requirements, or key management protocols based on public key certificates.

ISO 27100

ISO 27100 offers a concise overview of cybersecurity concepts, explaining their relevance and distinguishing them from information security. It also sets the context for cybersecurity.

ISO 27102

ISO 27102 provides guidelines for considering cyber-insurance as a risk treatment option to manage the impact of cyber-incidents within an organization's information security risk management framework.
It includes guidelines for:
- Considering the purchase of cyber-insurance to share cyber-risks.
- Using cyber-insurance to manage the impact of a cyber-incident.
- Sharing data and information between the insured and the insurer to support underwriting, monitoring, and claims activities related to a cyber-insurance policy.
- Leveraging an information security management system when sharing relevant data and information with an insurer.

ISO 27103

ISO 27103 explains how ISO 27xxx and other ISO and IEC standards can be applied to cybersecurity.

ISO 27110

ISO 27110 is a guideline on developing cybersecurity frameworks.

ISO 27400

ISO 27400 addresses security and privacy for the Internet of Things (IoT).

ISO 27402

ISO 27402 specifies baseline information security and privacy controls for IoT devices.

ISO 27403

ISO 27403 provides guidelines for analyzing security and privacy risks and identifies controls for implementation in Internet of Things (IoT) domotics systems.

ISO 27550

ISO 27550 provides privacy engineering guidelines to help organizations incorporate recent advances in privacy engineering into system life cycle processes and covers: 1. The relationship between privacy engineering and other engineering disciplines (system engineering, security engineering, risk management), 2. Privacy engineering activities in essential processes such as knowledge management, risk management, requirement analysis, and architecture design.

ISO 27551

ISO 27551 will outline the requirements for Attribute-Based Unlinkable Entity Authentication (ABUEA).

ISO 27553-1

ISO 27553-1 provides high-level security and privacy requirements and recommendations for biometric authentication on mobile devices. It includes guidelines for functional components and communication security and privacy. This document is applicable to scenarios where biometric data and derived biometric data remain on the device, operating in local modes only.

ISO 27554

ISO 27554 provides guidelines for managing identity-related risk, extending the principles of ISO 31000. It utilizes the ISO 31000 process to help users establish context and assess risk, offering risk scenarios for processes and implementations exposed to identity-related risk. This document applies to risk assessment for processes and services dependent on or related to identity, excluding aspects of risk associated with general delivery, technology, or security issues.

ISO 27555

ISO 27555 is intended for use by organizations where PII is stored or processed and offers guidance on deleting personal data (PII) by specifying:
- Harmonized terminology for PII deletion.
- An efficient approach for defining deletion rules.
- Required documentation.
- Broad definitions of roles, responsibilities, and processes.

ISO 27555 does not address:
- Specific legal provisions as mandated by national law or specified in contracts.
- Specific deletion rules for particular PII clusters defined by PII controllers.
- Deletion mechanisms.

- Reliability, security, and suitability of deletion mechanisms.
- Specific techniques for de-identification of data.

ISO 27556

ISO 27556 establishes a framework for managing and sharing users' privacy preferences.

ISO 27557

ISO 27557 advises using ISO 31000 to manage privacy risks and provides guidance for integrating personally identifiable information (PII) processing risks into an organizational privacy risk management program. It differentiates between the impact of PII processing on individuals and potential consequences for organizations, such as reputational damage. The document guides incorporating organizational consequences of adverse privacy impacts on individuals and privacy events that harm the organization without causing individual privacy impacts. ISO 27557 helps implement a risk-based privacy program integrated into the organization's overall risk management.

ISO 27559

ISO 27559 provides a framework for de-identifying (anonymizing) personal data. It outlines methods for identifying and mitigating re-identification risks and managing risks associated with the lifecycle of de-identified data. This standard is applicable to all types and sizes of organizations, including public and private companies, government entities, and not-for-profit organizations. It is designed for PII controllers and PII processors acting on a controller's behalf, who implement data de-identification processes to enhance privacy.

ISO 27560

ISO 27560 defines an interoperable, open, and extensible information structure for recording privacy consent records. It provides requirements and recommendations for using consent receipts and records related to PII principals' consent for PII processing. The standard supports providing a record of consent to the PII principal, exchanging consent information between systems, and managing the lifecycle of recorded consent. In summary, ISO 27560 offers a standardized framework for documenting, exchanging, and managing privacy consent records.

ISO 27561

ISO 27561 outlines a privacy engineering approach to determine and meet privacy-related requirements. It operationalizes the privacy principles from ISO 29100 into controls and functional capabilities using a process based on ISO 24774. Designed for use with relevant privacy and security standards, it supports networked, interdependent systems. This document is intended for engineers and practitioners developing systems that control or process personally identifiable information.

ISO 27563

ISO 27563 addresses the security and privacy implications of various Artificial Intelligence use cases, building on those published in ISO 24030. It outlines best practices for assessing security and privacy in AI systems, covering:
- Overall assessment of security and privacy in the AI system.
- Security and privacy concerns.
- Security and privacy risks.
- Security and privacy controls.
- Security and privacy assurance.
- Security and privacy plans.

ISO 27570

ISO 27570 provides privacy guidance for smart cities from a multi-agency and citizen-centric perspective. It covers:
- Privacy protection in the smart city ecosystem.
- Using standards globally and organizationally for citizens' benefit.
- Processes for smart city ecosystem privacy protection.

This standard applies to all types and sizes of organizations, including public and private companies, government entities, and not-for-profit organizations involved in smart city services.

ISO 27701

ISO 27701 is one of the most popular standards these days and specifies requirements and offers guidance for extending an ISO 27001 ISMS to manage both privacy and information security. It provides a framework for establishing, implementing, maintaining, and continually improving a Privacy Information Management System (PIMS) as an extension to ISO 27001 and ISO 27002. It outlines PIMS-related requirements and guidance for PII controllers and processors responsible for PII processing. ISO 27701 applies to all types and sizes of organizations, including public and private companies, government entities, and not-for-profit organizations, that process PII within an ISMS.

ISO 27799

ISO 27799 provides health sector-specific ISMS implementation guidance based on ISO 27002. It includes:
- **Guidelines for Health Informatics**: Supports the interpretation and implementation of ISO 27002 within health informatics, supplementing it where needed.
- **Implementation Guidance**: Details on implementing ISO 27002 controls to ensure the confidentiality, integrity, and availability of personal health information.

- **Scope of Health Information**: Applies to all forms of health information, regardless of medium or transmission method, ensuring appropriate protection.
- **Technology-Neutral**: Accommodates rapid technological changes, allowing for new or developing technologies.
- **Exclusions**: Does not cover anonymization methodologies, pseudonymization methodologies, network quality of service, and data quality (distinct from data integrity).

ISO 27799, along with ISO 27002, defines the necessary information security requirements for healthcare but does not specify how to meet these requirements. Understanding ISO 27002 is essential for comprehending ISO 27799.

ISO 27000:2018

ISO 27000 is a free of charge 34-page document entitled *"Information technology — Security techniques — Information security management systems — Overview and vocabulary"* and has three main goals:

1. Provide an overview to the important standards in ISO 27xxx family of Information Security Management Systems (ISMS)-related standards.
2. Introduce and define the information security management system.
3. Provide a glossary/vocabulary of the terms used throughout the ISO 27xxx family of standard.

Unlike other documents in the ISO 27xxx family of standard, you can download an English or French digital copy of ISO 27001:2018 standard free of charge from ISO/IEC Information Technology Task Force (ITTF) web site at https://standards.iso.org/ittf/PubliclyAvailableStandards/index.html

Glossary

In the context of ISO 27xxx, you face uncommon usage of auxiliary verbs! So as of now, we have to adapt ourselves with the following ISO 27xxx grammar rules:

- "shall" indicates a requirement in ISO 27xxx standards!
- "should" indicates a recommendation in ISO 27xxx standards.
- "may" indicates a permission in ISO 27xxx standards.
- "can" indicates a possibility or a capability in ISO 27xxx standards.

Other useful and important terms and definitions that are described in ISO 27000:2018 are as follows:

- Access Control: Means to ensure that access to assets is authorized and restricted based on business and security requirements.
- Attack: Attempt to destroy, expose, alter, disable, steal or gain unauthorized access to or make unauthorized use of an asset.
- Audit: Systematic, independent and documented process for obtaining audit evidence and evaluating it objectively to determine the extent to which the audit criteria are fulfilled. Audit can be either an internal or an external audit. An internal audit is conducted by the organization itself, or by an external party on its behalf.
- Audit Scope: Extent and boundaries of an audit.
- Authentication: Provision of assurance that a claimed characteristic of an entity is correct.
- Availability: Property of being accessible and usable on demand by an authorized entity.
- Competence: Ability to apply knowledge and skills to achieve intended results.
- Confidentiality: Property that information is not made available or disclosed to unauthorized individuals, entities, or processes.

- Continual Improvement: Recurring activity to enhance performance.
- Control or Information Security Control: Measure that is modifying risk. Controls include any process, policy, device, practice, or other actions which modify risk.
- Correction: Action to eliminate a detected nonconformity.
- Corrective Action: Action to eliminate the cause of a nonconformity and to prevent recurrence.
- Documented Information: Information required to be controlled and maintained by an organization and the medium on which it is contained. Documented information can be in any format and media and from any source.
- Effectiveness: Extent to which planned activities are realized and planned results achieved.
- Information Security: Preservation of confidentiality, integrity and availability of information. In addition, other properties, such as authenticity, accountability, non-repudiation, and reliability can also be involved.
- Information Security Continuity: Processes and procedures for ensuring continued information security operations.
- information Security Event: Identified occurrence of a system, service or network state indicating a possible breach of information security policy or failure of controls, or a previously unknown situation that can be security relevant.
- Information Security Incident: Single or a series of unwanted or unexpected information security events that have a significant probability of compromising business operations and threatening information security.
- Information Security Incident Management: Set of processes for detecting, reporting, assessing, responding to, dealing with, and learning from information security incidents.
- Information Security Management System (ISMS) Professional: Person who establishes, implements,

maintains and continuously improves one or more information security management system processes.

- Information System: Set of applications, services, information technology assets, or other information-handling components.
- Integrity: Property of accuracy and completeness.
- Interested Party or Stakeholder: Person or organization that can affect, be affected by, or perceive itself to be affected by a decision or activity.
- Level of Risk: Magnitude of a risk expressed in terms of the combination of consequences and their likelihood.
- Management System: Set of interrelated or interacting elements of an organization to establish policies and objectives and processes to achieve those objectives. A management system can address a single discipline or several disciplines. The system elements include the organization's structure, roles and responsibilities, planning and operation. The scope of a management system may include the whole of the organization, specific and identified functions of the organization, specific and identified sections of the organization, or one or more functions across a group of organizations.
- Nonconformity: Non-fulfilment of a requirement
- Non-repudiation: Ability to prove the occurrence of a claimed event or action and its originating entities.
- Policy: Intentions and direction of an organization by its top management.
- Process: Set of interrelated or interacting activities which transforms inputs into outputs.
- Requirement: Need or expectation that is stated, generally implied or obligatory. "Generally implied" means that it is custom or common practice for the organization and interested parties that the need or expectation under consideration is implied.
- Residual Risk or Retained Risk: Risk remaining after risk treatment.
- Review: Activity undertaken to determine the suitability, adequacy and effectiveness of the subject matter to achieve established objectives.

- Risk: Effect of uncertainty on objectives. An effect is a deviation from the expected, positive or negative. Uncertainty is the state, even partial, of deficiency of information related to, understanding or knowledge of, an event, its consequence, or likelihood. In the context of information security management systems, information security risks can be expressed as an effect of uncertainty on information security objectives. Information security risk is associated with the potential that threats will exploit vulnerabilities of an information asset or group of information assets and thereby cause harm to an organization.
- Risk Acceptance: Informed decision to take a particular risk. Risk acceptance can occur without risk treatment or during the process of risk treatment. Accepted risks are subject to monitoring and review.
- Risk Assessment: Overall process of risk identification, risk analysis and risk evaluation.
- Risk Evaluation: Process of comparing the results of risk analysis with risk criteria to determine whether the risk and/or its magnitude is acceptable or tolerable. Risk evaluation assists in the decision about risk treatment.
- Risk Identification: Process of finding, recognizing and describing risks. Risk identification involves the identification of risk sources, events, their causes and their potential consequences. Risk identification can involve historical data, theoretical analysis, informed and expert opinions, and stakeholders' needs.
- Risk Management: Coordinated activities to direct and control an organization with regard to risk.
- Risk Treatment: Process to modify risk. Risk treatment can involve:
    - Avoiding the risk by deciding not to start or continue with the activity that gives rise to the risk.
    - Taking or increasing risk in order to pursue an opportunity.
    - Removing the risk source.

- Changing the likelihood.
- Changing the consequences.
- Sharing the risk with another party or parties (including contracts and risk financing).
- Retaining the risk by informed choice
- Threat: Potential cause of an unwanted incident, which can result in harm to a system or organization.
- Top Management: Person or group of people who directs and controls an organization at the highest level. Top management has the power to delegate authority and provide resources within the organization. If the scope of the management system covers only part of an organization, then top management refers to those who direct and control that part of the organization.
- Vulnerability: Weakness of an asset or control that can be exploited by one or more threats.

For the full list please visit the ISO 27000:2018 standard, page 1 to 11.

Successful Implementation of an ISMS

According to ISO 27000:2018, The following fundamental principles contribute to the successful implementation of an ISMS:

- Awareness of the need for information security.
- Assignment of responsibility for information security.
- Incorporating management commitment and the interests of stakeholders.
- Enhancing societal values.
- Risk assessments determine appropriate controls to reach acceptable levels of risk.
- Security incorporated as an essential element of information networks and systems.
- Active prevention and detection of information security incidents.
- Ensuring a comprehensive approach to information

security management.

- Continual reassessment of information security and making of modifications as appropriate.

ISO 27002: 2022

ISO 27002 is a complementary standard to ISO 27001, providing guidelines and best practices for information security controls. It offers a detailed set of controls and implementation guidance to help organizations protect their information assets and manage information security risks effectively. As of today, the latest version of ISO 27002 is ISO/IEC 27002:2022, which was published in February 2022. It includes updates to align with the evolving landscape of information security threats and best practices.

As mentioned before, ISO 27002 provides a comprehensive set of guidelines for selecting, implementing, and managing information security controls. These controls are organized into four domains,

1. **Organizational Controls:** Guidelines for establishing and maintaining an effective information security management framework.
2. **People Controls:** Guidance on managing human resources and security awareness training.
3. **Physical Controls:** Measures to protect physical assets and environments.
4. **Technical Controls:** Best practices for securing IT systems, networks, and data.

ISO 27002 covers several domains and various aspects of information security such as:

- **Access Control:** Policies for managing user access to information and systems.
- **Cryptography:** Guidelines for using cryptographic techniques to protect information.
- **Physical and Environmental Security:** Measures to protect against physical threats and environmental risks.

- **Operations Security:** Procedures for managing and maintaining secure operations.
- **Communications Security:** Practices for securing communications and information exchange.
- **System Acquisition, Development, and Maintenance:** Guidelines for secure software development and maintenance.
- **Supplier Relationships:** Managing information security risks in third-party relationships.
- **Incident Management:** Processes for identifying, reporting, and responding to security incidents.
- **Business Continuity Management:** Ensuring the availability of critical information and systems during disruptions.
- **Compliance:** Guidelines for ensuring adherence to legal, regulatory, and contractual requirements.

Organizations cannot be certified specifically for ISO 27002. ISO 27002 is designed to support ISO 27001 by providing additional guidance on implementing the controls mentioned in Annex A of ISO 27001. Certification is available for ISO 27001 but not ISO 27000 or ISO 27002.

So, organizations can use ISO 27002 to enhance their information security practices and support their ISO 27001 certification efforts. By following the optional guidelines in ISO 27002, organizations can better ensure that their information security controls are robust, effective, and aligned with best practices, thereby facilitating their compliance with ISO 27001 requirements.

Claim ISO 27001 Compliance

ISO/IEC 27001:2022 is an international standard written by the International Organization for Standardization which outlines the requirements for implementing an Information Security Management System (ISMS). Organizations can claim compliance with this standard by implementing an information security program, called ISMS in the context of ISO 27001, that meets the requirements outlined in the standard and then passing an independent certification audit.

Implementation of an ISMS involves a combination of technology, processes, and policies to secure information assets and ensure its confidentiality, integrity and availability. This can include measures such as password management, firewalls, encryption, regular security updates and much more. The final goal of almost all information security programs is keeping sensitive information safe and secure in order to prevent breaches and protect against various cyber threats including but not limited to phishing attacks, malware attacks, DDoS attacks, SQL injection attacks, Man-in-the-Middle (MitM) attacks, Advanced Persistent Threats (APT) attacks, watering hole attacks, social engineering attacks, Zero-Day exploits, cryptojackings, and insider threats.

Steps to Claim Compliance with ISO 27001

- **Implement an ISMS:** Organizations must develop and implement an ISMS that meets the requirements outlined in ISO 27001 standard. Organizations do that by developing and implementing policies, procedures, and security controls for information security, cybersecurity and privacy protection.
- **Conduct a self-assessment:** Organizations should conduct a self-assessment to ensure that their implementation of policies, procedures, and controls meets the requirements of ISO 27001 standard by documenting different aspects of their ISMS and its security controls, testing the security controls, and finally evaluating the effectiveness of their ISMS. This process is called **Internal Audit** in the context of ISO 27xxx family of standards.
- **Obtain certification:** Organizations seeking ISO 27001 can obtain their ISO certification by undergoing an independent certification audit by a third-party certification body. The certification body conducts an audit to verify that the implemented ISMS meets the

requirements of the ISO 27001 standard.

- **Maintain compliance:** The compliant organizations must regularly review and update their ISMS in order to ensure that it is still relevant and effective. The organization must also undergo annual **surveillance audits** to ensure that they are still compliant with the standard.

What is New in ISO 27001?

To us, ISO 27001:2022 does not significantly differ from ISO 27001:2013 in terms of its core requirements. However, there are some notable changes, particularly in the suggested controls listed in Annex A.

Change in the Title

The title of the standard has been changed from "*Information technology — Security techniques — Information security management systems — Requirements*" to "*Information security, cybersecurity and privacy protection — Information security management systems — Requirements*"

The title of Annex A of ISO 27001 standard has also been changed from "*Reference control objectives and controls*" to "*Information security controls reference*".

Changes in the Planning Clause

Information security objectives and planning to achieve them must now be "available as documented information".

In 6.1.3 c subsection, the notes have been revised. "Control" is replaced with "information security control" and the control objectives get deleted.

And a new section has been added under the Planning clause entitled "*6.3 Planning of changes*". This new subsection does not specify any crystal-clear process that must be included in your ISMS. The new subsection just asks for a planned change when it comes to the need for a change to ISMS.

Change in the Support Clause

The requirements to define who shall communicate and the item for effecting communication have been replaced by a new requirement to define "how to communicate". It is under the *Communication* subsection.

Changes in the Operation Clause

The requirement to plan how to achieve information security objectives has been updated with a new language which asks for establishing criteria for the processes and implementing control of the processes in accordance with the established criteria.

In the new version of ISO 27001 standard, it is mandatory that the organizations control *"externally provided processes, products or services relevant to the information security management system"* rather than just processes. The previous version of ISO 27001, had another language for that which just covered only the processes: *"The organization shall ensure that outsourced processes are determined and controlled."*

Changes in the Performance Evaluation Clause

In the new version of the standard, methods of monitoring, measurement, analysis and evaluating the effectiveness of the ISMS should be *"comparable and reproducible"*. The previous version just asked to have methods of monitoring, measurement, analysis and evaluation in place and did talk about the characteristics of those methods.

The management review inputs must now also consider changes in the needs and expectations of interested parties which are relevant to the information
security management system. This is a brand-new item under *"9.3.2 Management review inputs" subsection.*

Changes in the Annex A

Annex A has been revised completely to be fully aligned with the new version of ISO 27002 which was released before ISO

27001:2022.

Some ISO 27001 controls have been merged or removed, and we see some new controls. The 2022 version of ISO 27001 lists 93 controls instead of 114 controls in ISO 27001:2013.

New controls fall under four themes rather than fourteen clauses (Clause A.5 to Clause A.18) that we had in ISO 27001:2013.

New themes of controls in ISO 27001:2022 are:

1. People (8 controls)
2. Organizational (37 controls)
3. Technological (34 controls)
4. Physical (14 controls)

The new controls are in the following areas:

- Threat Intelligence (5.7)
- Information Security for Use of Cloud Services (5.23)
- ICT Readiness for Business Continuity (5.30)
- Physical Security Monitoring (7.1)
- Configuration Management (8.9)
- Information Deletion (8.10)
- Data Masking (8.11)
- Data Leakage Prevention (8.12)
- Monitoring Activities (8.16)
- Web Filtering (8.23)
- Secure Coding (8.28)

Theme is not the only new concept in ISO 27001/27002 controls. New ISO 27001/27002 controls also come with five types of attributes to create different views which are different categorizations of controls as seen from a different perspective to the themes. You do not see these kinds of details in ISO 27001 standard. They are not listed in ISO 27001:2022 but you can find them in ISO 27002:2022.

New attributes of controls in ISO 27002:2022 are:

1. Control Type (Preventive, Detective, and Corrective)
2. Information Security Properties (Confidentiality, Integrity, and Availability)
3. Cybersecurity Concepts (Identify, Protect, Detect, Respond, and Recover)
4. Operational Capabilities (Governance, Asset_management, Information_protection, Human_resource_security, Physical_security, System_and_network_security, Application_security, Secure_configuration, Identity_and_access_management, Threat_and_vulnerability_management, Continuity, upplier_relationships_security, Legal_and_compliance, information_security_event_management and Information_security_assurance)
5. Security Domains (Governance and Ecosystem, Protection, Defense, and Resilience)

The above-mentioned attributes of ISO 27001/ISO 27002 security controls are generic enough to be used in different types of organizations. Organizations may disregard one or more of the attributes or they can create attributes of their own in order to create their own organizational views. By the way, this is not a mandatory requirement for getting certified for ISO 27001.

Transition from 2013 Version to 2022 Version

For ISO 27001 certified organizations, there is a three-year transition period to revise their ISMS to meet the requirements of the 2022 version of ISO 27001, so there might be plenty of time for the organizations to apply the necessary changes described in ISO 27001:2022. The problem is that not all certification bodies offer the 2013 version of certification anymore. So, I believe it is worth checking with your certification body if you need to start the transition sooner than later. It is highly recommended not to leave your due diligence till the last minute to comply with the new ISO requirements, so if you are due to renew your certification during the transition period, you'd better work against the new set of information security controls of ISO 27001/27002.

If an organization has designed and/or implemented their ISMS based on ISO 27001:2013 requirements and guidelines, auditors in the transition audit, whether it is internal audit or external audit, rely on the document review, especially for reviewing the technological controls, check the updated version of the Statement of Applicability (SoA), check the updated version of risk treatment plan, and the most important, effective implementation of the controls based on the new control descriptions in the ISO 27001:2022.

So, the organizations should include the following critical steps for their transitions:
1. Gap analysis of ISO 27001:2022 version and adapt the changes to their Information Security Management System (ISMS).
2. Update their statement of applicability (SoA) based on the new control descriptions in the ISO 27001:2022.
3. Ensure that their documents, especially the organization's risk assessment document and risk treatment plan is updated.
4. Effective implementation of the new controls.

What is New in ISO 27006-1:2024?

As discussed in the previous chapter, ISO 27006 is a standard within the ISO 27xxx series that provides guidelines for certification bodies and auditors on how to audit an ISMS. The updated standard ISO/IEC 27006-1:2024 introduces a few key changes, particularly in how certification bodies should account for the number of personnel within organizations. This adjustment could reduce the number of audit days that certification bodies can justify charging for.

Another significant change is the shift from requiring a pre-certification audit to requiring solid evidence of an active certification and maintenance plan. This plan must include internal audits, management reviews, and other ongoing processes. At the time of certification, it's not enough to simply claim that an audit has been conducted; there must be demonstrable evidence of a structured plan that is actively maintained throughout the certification period.

The new requirement states: "The certification body shall not certify an ISMS unless there is sufficient evidence to demonstrate that arrangements for management reviews and internal ISMS audits have been implemented, are effective, and will be maintained covering the scope of certification."

2024 Update of ISO 27001

In response to a directive from the ISO/IEC Joint Technical Committee, ISO has published an amendment in 2024 titled *"AMENDMENT 1: Climate Action Changes."* Which is available at https://www.iso.org/obp/ui/en/#iso:std:iso-iec:27001:ed-3:v1:amd:1:v1:en free of charge.

This amendment introduces two key updates to ISO 27001:2022:
- It mandates that compliant organizations assess whether climate change is a relevant concern.
- It acknowledges that relevant interested parties may have requirements related to climate change.

While ISO 27001 may not seem directly related to climate change, this amendment applies to all ISO management system standards. There is, in fact, a significant connection between climate change and security.

Availability, one of the three pillars of information security, can be threatened by climate-related events. For instance, if your servers are located near water, the increased risk of flooding due to climate change could compromise both the availability and integrity of your data and services.

It's essential not to underestimate the security risks posed by non-malicious threats—they can be just as damaging as those from malicious actors.

Structure of ISO 27001

ISO 27001 standard has two major parts: The mandatory clauses (Clause 0 to Clause 10) and the Annex A of the standard which contain 93 information security controls fall under 4 categories.

Mandatory Clauses

There are 11 mandatory clauses in ISO 27001:2022 starting from clause 0. In the first four clauses, we will face a kind of general metadata of the standard. These four clauses provide general information about the standard:

- Clause 0: Introduction
- Clause 1: Scope
- Clause 2: Normative References
- Clause 3: Terms and Definitions

The following clauses, 4 to 10 are mandatory requirements as indicated in the standard:

Important Note: *Excluding any of the requirements specified in Clauses 4 to 10 is* **not** *acceptable when an organization claims conformity to ISO 27001.*

So, if your company is aiming to get ISO 27001:2022 certification, these are the required processes, procedures, documents, policies and tools which are needed to be included in order to deliver an ISO 27001 compliant information security management system:

- Clause 4: Context of the Organization
  - 4.1 Understanding the Organization and Its Context
  - 4.2 Understanding the Needs and Expectations of Interested Parties
  - 4.3 Determining the Scope of the Information Security Management System

- 4.4 Information Security Management System
- Cluse 5: Leadership
  - 5.1 Leadership and Commitment
  - 5.2 Policy
  - 5.3 Organizational Roles, Responsibilities and Authorities
- Clause 6: Planning
  - 6.1 Actions to Address Risks and Opportunities
    - 6.1.1 General
    - 6.1.2 Information Security Risk Assessment
    - 6.1.3 Information Security Risk Treatment
  - 6.2 Information Security Objectives and Planning to Achieve Them
  - 6.3 Planning of changes
- Clause 7: Support
  - 7.1 Resources
  - 7.2 Competence
  - 7.3 Awareness
  - 7.4 Communication
  - 7.5 Documented Information
    - 7.5.1 General
    - 7.5.2 Creating and Updating
    - 7.5.3 Control of Documented Information
- Clause 8: Operation
  - 8.1 Operational Planning and Control
  - 8.2 Information Security Risk Assessment
  - 8.3 Information Security Risk Treatment
- Clause 9: Performance Evaluation
  - 9.1 Monitoring, Measurement, Analysis and Evaluation
  - 9.2 Internal Audit
    - 9.2.1 General
    - 9.2.2 Internal Audit Program
  - 9.3 Management Review

- 9.3.1 General
- 9.3.2 Management Review Inputs
- 9.3.3 Management Review Results
- Clause 10: Improvement
  - 10.1 Continual Improvement
  - 10.2 Nonconformity and Corrective Action

Annex A

Annex A of ISO 27001:2022 lists 93 information security controls to provide a framework that forms the basis of your organization's **Statement of Applicability (SoA)**. Although no controls have been removed from the previous version, ISO 27001:2022 lists only 93 controls compared to the 114 in ISO 27001:2013. This reduction is due to merging 56 controls into 24. Additionally, as mentioned before, these controls are now organized into 4 themes instead of the previous 14 clauses.

These 93 controls fall under four themes/categories/clauses:
- Organizational Controls
- People Controls
- Physical Controls
- Technological Controls

Although the Annex A controls are somewhat self-explanatory, for the detailed information about each control, you can refer to their comprehensive explanation in ISO 27002:2022 standard. Bear in mind that these controls are not mandatory like mandatory clauses of the standard i.e. clause 4 to clause 10 of ISO 27001.

It is a common misconception that all security controls listed in Annex A of the ISO 27001 standard must be implemented to achieve ISO 27001 certification. Instead, organizations should specify in the Statement of Applicability (SoA) which controls are relevant and necessary based on their risk management processes and management decisions. In other words, only those security controls that address the specific needs and risks of your business should be implemented.

Determining which controls are necessary requires thorough risk assessment and risk treatment processes. This analysis can be time-consuming but is essential for ensuring that security measures are tailored to your organization's unique requirements. The goal is not to implement security measures indiscriminately or to strive to become the most secure organization in the world, but to achieve a level of security that adequately addresses your business risks.

Risk assessment and risk treatment are crucial for identifying which security controls are needed. These processes help prioritize and implement the controls that will most effectively protect your organization's assets and support its business objectives.

ISO 27001 Requirements

Clause 4.1, Issues

The organization must identify both external and internal issues that are relevant to its purpose and impact its capability to achieve the desired outcomes of its information security management system.

In the context of ISO 27001, "internal issues" and "external issues" refer to various factors and conditions within and outside the organization that can influence its ability to achieve the objectives of its Information Security Management System (ISMS). Understanding these issues helps the organization identify potential risks and opportunities related to information security.

Internal Issues

Internal issues are factors within the organization that can impact its information security. These may include but not limited to:

1. **Organizational Structure**: The way the organization is structured, including roles, responsibilities, and reporting lines.
2. **Policies and Procedures**: Existing policies, procedures, and practices related to information security.
3. **Resources and Capabilities**: Availability of financial, technological, and human resources.
4. **Culture and Values**: The organization's culture and its commitment to security practices.
5. **Processes and Systems**: Internal processes, systems, and technologies used for managing and protecting information.
6. **Historical Data**: Past security incidents and their impacts.
7. **Physical Environment**: Physical locations and their security controls.

External Issues

External issues are factors outside the organization that can affect its information security. These may include but not limited to:

1. **Legal and Regulatory Requirements**: Laws, regulations, and compliance requirements relevant to information security.
2. **Market Conditions**: The economic environment, including competition and market trends.
3. **Technological Developments**: Advances in technology that could impact information security.
4. **Socio-Cultural Factors**: Social and cultural trends that could influence security practices and awareness.
5. **Political and Environmental Factors**: Political stability, environmental events, and other macro-level factors.
6. **Supply Chain and Third Parties**: Relationships with suppliers, vendors, and other third parties that may have access to information.
7. **Industry Standards and Best Practices**: Standards, frameworks, and best practices relevant to the industry

Clause 4.2, Internal & External Parties

In the context of ISO 27001, interested parties or "internal parties" and "external parties" refer to the various stakeholders that can influence or be affected by an organization's information security management system (ISMS). Understanding these parties and their relevant requirements is crucial for implementing an effective ISMS. Per ISO 27001, "the requirements of interested parties can include legal and regulatory requirements and contractual obligations."

Internal Parties

Internal parties are stakeholders within the organization. They

may include:
1. **Employees**: Staff members at all levels who handle or interact with information assets.
2. **Management**: Leadership and management teams responsible for setting policies, procedures, and ensuring compliance.
3. **IT Department**: Individuals responsible for maintaining the technical infrastructure and security measures.
4. **Security Teams**: Personnel specifically tasked with implementing and managing security controls.
5. **Business Units**: Different departments or units within the organization that rely on secure information to operate effectively.

External Parties

External parties are stakeholders outside the organization. They may include:
1. **Customers**: Clients who expect their data to be protected and who may have specific security requirements.
2. **Suppliers and Vendors**: Third-party service providers who may have access to the organization's information or systems.
3. **Regulators and Auditors**: Government agencies and other bodies that enforce legal and regulatory requirements.
4. **Partners**: Business partners and affiliates who share information or collaborate on projects.
5. **Contractors**: Independent contractors or consultants who may access the organization's information or systems.
6. **Shareholders**: Investors who have an interest in the organization's compliance and overall security posture.

The organization must also identify the requirements of these interested parties and which of these requirements will be addressed by the information security management system.

Clause 4.3, Documented Scope

This is one of the most important parts of the ISO 27001 implementation and any other compliance frameworks like PCI-DSS or FedRAMP. As mentioned before, defining the boundaries and applicability of the information security management system is required to establish the scope. The considerations in determining the scope includes the external and internal issues as well as the interfaces and dependencies between activities performed by the organization, and those that are performed by other organizations. The ISO 27001 scope statement may cover what your organization does, what important information is covered by the ISMS and why security is important for your organization and finally, which parts of your organization are to be certified.

Bear in mind that the scope of an ISMS must be documented per ISO 27001.

Here are some examples of ISO/IEC 27001 scope statements:
1. **Example 1: IT Services Company**
   o Scope: "The ISMS covers all information assets, processes, and services managed by the IT department, including data centers, cloud services, network infrastructure, and support services at the headquarters located in San Francisco, CA. and two other locations for data centers: San Jose, CA and Las Vegas, NV."
2. **Example 2: Financial Institution (Bank)**
   o Scope: "The ISMS applies to the management of customer financial data, transaction processing systems, and associated support functions within the bank's main office and regional branches in North America."
3. **Example 3: Healthcare Provider**
   o Scope: "The ISMS encompasses all patient information management systems, electronic health records (EHR), and related support services at the main hospital and all affiliated clinics within the state of Texas.

4. **Example 4: Manufacturing Company**
   o Scope: "The ISMS includes all production control systems, supply chain management processes, and associated IT infrastructure at the main manufacturing facility and distribution center in Detroit, MI."
5. **Example 5: E-commerce Business**
   o Scope: "The ISMS covers the protection of customer data, payment processing systems, and e-commerce platform operations managed from the company's headquarters and data centers in New York, NY."
6. **Example 6: Government Agency**
   o Scope: "The ISMS applies to the management of confidential government records, communication systems, and support services within the agency's central office and all regional offices across the country."

These examples demonstrate how the scope of ISO 27001 can vary depending on the nature of the organization, its products, its processes, and/or the specific information assets that need protection. As you see in the above example, the scope is clearly defined to ensure that all relevant aspects of the organization's ISMS are covered and adequately protected. The scope statement will show up in your ISO 27001 certification.

Clause 4.4, ISMS

As you understood, the main purpose of ISO 27001 is to establish, implement, maintain, and continually improve an Information Security Management System (ISMS). An ISMS is a systematic approach to managing sensitive company information so that it remains secure. It encompasses people, processes, and IT systems by applying a risk management process. Clause 4.4 is talking about this important concept.

Clause 5.1, Commitment of the Leaders

One of the most important requirements of ISO 27001 is that the organization's senior management must demonstrate leadership and commitment to the information security management system by:

1. Ensuring that the information security policy and objectives are established and aligned with the organization's strategic direction.
2. Integrating the information security management system requirements into the organization's processes.
3. Providing the necessary resources for the information security management system.
4. Communicating the importance of effective information security management and adherence to the information security management system requirements.
5. Ensuring the information security management system achieves its intended outcomes.
6. Directing and supporting individuals to contribute to the effectiveness of the information security management system.
7. Promoting continual improvement.
8. Supporting other relevant management roles in demonstrating their leadership as it pertains to their areas of responsibility.

Different types of evidence can be provided for this requirement during an ISO 27001 audit:

- Documented information security policy and objectives that covers all aspects of above-mentioned items.
- Meeting minutes where policy and objectives were discussed and approved.
- Alignment documents or strategy maps showing how information security objectives support the overall

strategic direction.
- Communications from top management endorsing the information security policy and objectives.
- Process documentation showing the integration of ISMS requirements.
- Examples of modified processes or procedures that now include information security considerations.
- Records of resource planning and allocation including budget records showing allocation of funds for information security
- Procurement records for security tools and services.
- Emails, newsletters, or internal memos, recorded speeches or videos, presentation materials from town hall meetings from top management emphasizing the importance of information security.
- Roles and responsibilities documents clearly defining ISMS-related duties.
- Performance appraisals or recognition programs acknowledging contributions to ISMS.
- Records of improvement initiatives related to information security.
- Results of continuous monitoring and improvement programs.
- Documentation showing delegation of ISMS responsibilities to other management roles.
- Examples of other managers' involvement in ISMS activities and initiatives.

Clause 5.2, Documented Policies

In implementing ISO 27001, senior management must establish information security policies that encompass various aspects of an ISMS. An ISO 27001 auditor will review these policies to ensure they address each and every of the following topics:
- Appropriateness to the purpose of the organization
- Inclusion of information security objectives or provision of a framework for setting these objectives
- Commitment to satisfying applicable information

security requirements

- Commitment to the continual improvement of the information security management system.

Additionally, the information security policies must:

- Be available as documented information.
- Be communicated within the organization.
- Be available to interested parties, as appropriate.

During an ISO 27001 audit, the auditor may verify if the information security policies are available as documented information, communicated within the organization, and available to interested parties as appropriate. Here are the types of evidence an auditor may request to confirm these requirements:

- Copies of the documented information security policies.
- Records in the organization's document management system or other systems that show the employees have proper access or permission to see the documents.
- Audit trails demonstrating how the documents are stored, accessed, and maintained.
- Emails or internal memos distributing the information security policies to staff.
- Meeting minutes or presentation materials from staff briefings where policies were discussed.
- Training records showing that employees have been trained on the information security policies.
- Posters, intranet posts, or other internal communications highlighting the policies.
- Feedback mechanisms (e.g., surveys or acknowledgments) confirming employees have read and understood the policies.
- Public-facing documents or website sections where relevant policies are published for relevant external stakeholders.
- Records of communications with relevant third parties (e.g., suppliers, customers) sharing the policies.
- Contracts or agreements referencing the information security policies.

- Procedures or logs showing how relevant external parties can request and obtain the policies.
- Access logs or other evidence demonstrating that interested parties have accessed or received the policies.

Clause 5.3, Roles & Responsibilities

Defining roles, responsibilities, and authorities is essential for implementing any management system, including an Information Security Management System (ISMS). In ISMS implementation, senior management must ensure that responsibilities and authorities for information security roles are assigned and communicated within the organization.

Top management must assign responsibility and authority to ensure that the information security management system conforms to the requirements of ISO 27001 and report on the performance of the information security management system to top management. Evidence an ISO 27001 auditor may ask for this requirement are:

- Organizational charts detailing roles and responsibilities related to information security.
- Job descriptions specifying information security duties.
- Documentation of delegated authorities and responsibilities.
- Meeting minutes or formal communications where roles and responsibilities were assigned.
- Internal memos, emails, or announcements communicating assigned responsibilities and authorities.
- Records of staff meetings or training sessions where roles and responsibilities were discussed.
- Employee handbooks or internal documentation outlining information security roles.
- Acknowledgments from employees confirming their understanding of their information security roles and responsibilities.

- Reports or dashboards summarizing the performance of the ISMS.
- Records of management review meetings where ISMS performance is discussed.
- Performance metrics and key performance indicators (KPIs) related to information security.

Clause 6.1.1, Risks & Opportunities

The organization must identify the risks and opportunities that need to be addressed in order to:
- Ensure the information security management system achieves its intended outcomes
- Prevent or reduce undesired effects
- Achieve continual improvement.
- The organization must plan
- Actions to address these risks and opportunities.
- How to integrate and implement these actions into its information security management system processes and evaluate their effectiveness.

Clause 6.1.2, Documented Risk Assessment

The organization must define, document and apply an information security risk assessment process that:
- Establishes and maintains information security risk criteria, including risk acceptance criteria (aka risk acceptance level) as well as the criteria for performing information security risk assessments. As an example, these criteria can include
    1. **Regular Intervals**: The organization may establish regular annual risk assessments so they can conduct risk assessments at least once a year to review and evaluate the existing information security posture, identify new risks, and update risk treatment plans.
    2. **Major IT Architectural Changes**: The organization

may also conduct risk assessment for system overhauls, when the organization undergoes significant changes in its IT infrastructure or architecture, such as adopting new technologies, systems, or major software updates. Infrastructure Expansion may be considered as another factor to conduct a non-regular risk assessment, when expanding the existing IT infrastructure like adding new servers, databases, or networks.

3. **Changes in Risk Landscape**: The organization may also conduct risk assessment following significant security incidents or breaches to assess the impact, identify vulnerabilities, and update mitigation strategies or when they face environmental changes like when there are changes in the external environment that could impact the organization's risk landscape, such as new regulatory requirements, changes in the threat landscape, or market conditions. Organizational changes can also be considered for a new risk assessment. I mean, when there are major changes within the organization, such as mergers, acquisitions, or significant shifts in business operations and processes, it can be a good time to do a risk assessment.

4. **New Projects or Services**: The organization may also conduct risk assessment before the launch of new projects or services that may introduce new risks or affect existing controls. Or when there are substantial modifications to existing services, including changes to service delivery models or service providers.

5. **Regulatory and Compliance Updates**: The organization may also conduct risk assessment to ensure compliance with new or updated regulations and standards that impact information security. The organization may consider conducting risk assessment prior to scheduled compliance audits to ensure all necessary controls are in place and functioning effectively.

- Ensures that repeated information security risk assessments produce consistent, valid, and comparable results

- Identifies information security risks by applying the information security risk assessment process to identify risks associated with the loss of confidentiality, integrity, and availability of information within the scope of the information security management system and identifying the risk owners
- Analyzes the information security risks by assessing the potential consequences that would result if the identified risks were to materialize, assessing the realistic likelihood of the occurrence of the identified risks, and determining the levels of risk
- Evaluates the information security risks by comparing the results of risk analysis with the established risk criteria and prioritizing the analyzed risks for risk treatment

To ensure compliance with ISO 27001 clause 6.1.2, an auditor may request the following types of evidence during an audit:

Information Security Risk Assessment Process Document: A documented process outlining how risk assessments are conducted, including methodologies, tools, and techniques used as well as some evidence that show the process is regularly reviewed and updated.

Risk Criteria Documentation: Documents detailing the risk acceptance criteria and the criteria for performing risk assessments. And maybe some evidence showing how these criteria were established and approved.

Risk Assessment Reports: Records of regular risk assessments, including annual assessments, assessments after major IT changes, and assessments following security incidents. These kinds of reports should include identified risks, risk owners, and the context of each risk.

Risk Registers: Comprehensive registers or logs that list all identified information security risks, their likelihood and potential impact on confidentiality, integrity, and availability, and the assigned risk owners. They may also ask for evidence that risk registers are regularly updated.

Risk Analysis Records: Documentation of the analysis process, including assessments of potential consequences, likelihood of occurrence, and risk levels. And questions about the use of quantitative or qualitative methods to analyze risks.

Risk Evaluation Records: Evidence of comparing analyzed risks with the established risk criteria.

Clause 6.1.3, Documented Risk Treatment

The organization must define, document, and apply an information security risk treatment process to:

Select Appropriate Risk Treatment Options

- Choose suitable information security risk treatment options based on the results of the risk assessment(s).

Determine Necessary Controls

- Identify and determine all controls required to implement the chosen information security risk treatment options. These controls can be designed by the organization or sourced from any relevant framework.

Compare with Annex A of ISO 27001

- Compare the identified controls with those listed in Annex A of ISO 27001 to ensure that no necessary controls have been omitted. Annex A provides a list of potential information security controls, but it is not exhaustive. Additional controls can be included if needed.

Produce a Statement of Applicability

- Create a document called Statement of Applicability that includes:
  - The necessary controls
  - Justification for including each control
  - Whether each necessary control has been implemented
  - Justification for excluding any Annex A controls

Formulate a Risk Treatment Plan

- Develop a comprehensive information security risk treatment plan.

Obtain Approval

- Secure approval from risk owners for the information security risk treatment plan and obtain their acceptance of the residual information security risks.

The information security risk assessment and treatment process can be aligned with the principles and generic guidelines provided in ISO 31000 or any other risk management framework. ISO 27001 does not prescribe a specific risk management methodology as long as the aforementioned requirements are satisfied.

Clause 6.2 & 6.3, Objectives & Planning

The organization must establish information security objectives at relevant functions and levels. These objectives should be designed to align with the overall strategic goals of the organization and to enhance its information security posture. By establishing and managing information security objectives in this structured manner, the organization can ensure that its

ISMS remains effective, responsive, and aligned with its overall strategic goals.

According to clause 6.2 of ISO 27001, the information security objectives shall:

Be Consistent with the Information Security Policy: Ensure that the objectives support and reinforce the principles outlined in the organization's information security policy.

Be Measurable (if Practicable): Define objectives in a way that allows their achievement to be measured, facilitating performance tracking and evaluation.

Consider Applicable Information Security Requirements: Incorporate relevant legal, regulatory, and contractual requirements, as well as the outcomes of risk assessments and risk treatment activities.

Be Monitored: Regularly review and track progress towards achieving the objectives to ensure they are being met and remain relevant.

Be Communicated: Ensure that information security objectives are clearly communicated to all relevant stakeholders within the organization.

Be Updated as Appropriate: Review and revise objectives periodically or as needed to respond to changes in the organization's environment, risk landscape, or strategic direction.

Be Documented: Maintain documented information on the established information security objectives to ensure transparency and accountability.

The organization must retain documented information on the information security objectives to provide evidence of their existence and to facilitate their monitoring and review.

Planning to Achieve Information Security Objectives

When planning how to achieve its information security objectives, the organization must determine:

What Will Be Done: Clearly define the actions and initiatives required to achieve each objective.

Resources Required: Identify the necessary resources, including personnel, technology, and financial resources, needed to achieve the objectives.

Responsibilities: Assign clear responsibilities to individuals or teams for executing the actions and achieving the objectives.

Timeline: Establish a timeframe for completing the actions and achieving the objectives, including key milestones and deadlines.

Evaluation of Results: Define how the outcomes will be evaluated to ensure that the objectives have been met and to measure the effectiveness of the actions taken.

Some Examples for ISMS Objectives

Objective 1: Improve Security Awareness Training

- **Measure:** Achieve 95% completion of annual security awareness training by all employees.
- **Monitoring:** Track training completion rates monthly and report them to senior management.

Objective 2: Reduce the Number of Security Incidents

- **Measure:** Decrease the number of recorded security incidents by 20% over the next 12 months.
- **Monitoring:** Monthly analysis of security incident reports and trend analysis to be presented at quarterly management reviews.

Objective 3: Enhance Access Control Mechanisms

- **Measure:** Achieve 100% compliance with role-based access control (RBAC) policies across all critical systems within 6 months.
- **Monitoring:** Regular audits of access control lists, with non-compliance incidents reported monthly.

Objective 4: Increase the Resilience of IT Systems

- **Measure:** Reduce unplanned downtime due to security breaches by 30% within the next 12 months.
- **Monitoring:** Track and report system availability and downtime incidents on a monthly basis.

Objective 6: Ensure Compliance with Regulatory Requirements

- **Measure:** Achieve 100% compliance with applicable information security regulations and standards during the next external audit.
- **Monitoring:** Monthly internal audits and review of compliance status, with results reported to the management team.

Managing Changes to the Information Security Management System

When the organization determines the need for changes to the information security management system (ISMS), the changes shall be carried out in a planned manner. In my opinion, a good plan should include:

- Assessing the potential impact of proposed changes on the ISMS and its objectives.
- Planning and implementing changes systematically to ensure they are integrated smoothly and effectively.
- Communicating changes to all relevant stakeholders to maintain awareness and understanding.

- Monitoring and reviewing the changes to confirm they achieve the desired outcomes and do not introduce new risks.

Clause 7.1, Determining the Resources

Clause 7.1 of ISO 27001 briefly addresses the resources needed for an ISMS, stating that the organization shall determine and provide the necessary resources for the establishment, implementation, maintenance, and continual improvement of the information security management system.

For this requirement, you may consider all or some of the following resources:

Human Resources

- Skilled personnel with expertise in information security, such as ISMS managers, security analysts, internal auditors and IT staff.
- Training and development programs to ensure staff are knowledgeable about information security policies, procedures, and best practices.

Technical Resources

- Hardware and software essential for implementing and maintaining security controls, including firewalls, intrusion detection systems, encryption tools, and security information and event management (SIEM) systems.
- Secure infrastructure for data storage, processing, and communication.

Financial Resources

- Budget allocations for acquiring, implementing, and maintaining security technologies and services.

- Funds for ongoing training, awareness programs, and incident response activities.

Physical Resources

- Secure physical locations and facilities to protect sensitive information and IT infrastructure.
- Access control systems to manage entry to restricted areas.

Information Resources

- Access to up-to-date security policies, standards, guidelines, and procedures.
- Security awareness materials and training content for employees.

Organizational Resources

- Defined roles and responsibilities for information security within the organization.
- Governance structures and committees to oversee the ISMS.

External Resources

- Third-party services such as security consultants, auditors, and managed security service providers (MSSPs).
- Partnerships with external entities for threat intelligence and security collaboration.
- External auditors who audit ISMS or are hired for other information security related audits like SOX IT audit, PCI-DSS audit and so on.

Clause 7.2, Competence

Clause 7.2 of ISO 27001, titled "Competence," outlines the

requirements for ensuring that individuals involved in an organization's information security management system (ISMS) possess the necessary skills and knowledge. This clause specifies that the organization must:

Determine Required Competence: Identify the necessary competence for individuals performing tasks under its control that affect information security performance.

Ensure Competence: Ensure these individuals are competent based on appropriate education, training, or experience.

Acquire and Evaluate Competence: When necessary, take actions to acquire the required competence and evaluate the effectiveness of these actions. This may include providing training, mentoring, reassigning current employees, or hiring or contracting competent individuals.

Document Competence: Retain appropriate documented information as evidence of the competence of individuals involved in the ISMS.

This clause of ISO 27001 emphasizes the importance of having skilled and knowledgeable personnel to maintain and improve the organization's information security posture. ISO 27001 believed that having skilled and knowledgeable staff requires organizations to understand and define the specific skills and knowledge required for roles that impact information security, verify that individuals possess the necessary qualifications, whether through formal education, relevant training programs, or practical experience, implement measures to bridge any competence gaps, such as organizing training sessions, providing mentorship, reassigning roles, or hiring new personnel with the required expertise. The effectiveness of these measures must be evaluated to ensure they meet the intended objectives and keep records that demonstrate the competence of individuals. This could include certificates, training records, resumes, or performance evaluations.

Clause 7.3, Awareness

Clause 7.3 of ISO 27001, titled "Awareness," mandates that all individuals performing work under the organization's control must be aware of the following:

Information Security Policy: Understand the organization's information security policy.

Contribution to ISMS Effectiveness: Recognize their role in contributing to the effectiveness of the information security management system (ISMS) and the benefits of enhanced information security performance.

Implications of Non-Conformance: Be aware of the consequences of not adhering to the information security management system requirements.

This clause of ISO 27001 emphasizes the importance of awareness among all in-scope personnel regarding their roles and responsibilities related to information security. It ensures that everyone involved is informed and understands how their actions impact the ISMS and overall information security. So, employees need to be familiar with the organization's information security policy, which outlines the principles and guidelines for maintaining information security. They also should understand how their specific roles and actions contribute to the effectiveness of the ISMS. They should be aware of the benefits that come from improved information security performance, such as reduced risks and enhanced protection of information assets. They also should be aware of the potential negative consequences if they do not comply with the ISMS requirements. ISO 27001 believes that this awareness helps reinforce the importance of following established procedures and policies to maintain a secure information environment.

Clause 7.4, Communication

Clause 7.4 of ISO 27001, titled "Communication," requires the organization to establish the need for internal and external communications related to the information security management system (ISMS). This includes determining:

What to Communicate: Identify the information that needs to be communicated regarding the ISMS.

When to Communicate: Determine the appropriate timing and frequency of these communications.

With Whom to Communicate: Specify the internal and external parties that need to receive the communications.

How to Communicate: Decide on the methods and channels for delivering the communications effectively.

This clause highlights the importance of structured and effective communication within and outside the organization to support the ISMS. It ensures that relevant information is shared in a timely, consistent, and clear manner. It wants the organizations to identify the specific information that needs to be communicated about the ISMS. This could include policies, procedures, risk assessments, security incidents, and updates. Organizations also need to determine when communications should occur. This includes setting regular intervals for routine updates as well as ad-hoc communications in response to specific events or changes. ISO 27001 also says that it is crucial that organizations identify the target audience for communications. This includes internal stakeholders such as employees, management, and departments, as well as external stakeholders such as clients, suppliers, regulatory bodies, and partners. Methods of communication is the last part of this topic in ISO 27001 indicating that the organizations must decide on the appropriate methods for delivering information. This could involve meetings, emails, reports, intranet postings, newsletters, or other communication tools and platforms.

Clause 7.5, Documentation, Documentation, Documentation!

Clause 7.5 of ISO 27001, titled "Documentation," is very crucial for the effective implementation and management of an information security management system (ISMS). This clause outlines the requirements for maintaining and controlling documented information within the ISMS.

General Requirements

The organization's ISMS must include:

Documented Information Required by ISO 27001: All documentation explicitly required by the ISO 27001 standard.

Additional Necessary Documentation: Any other documentation deemed necessary by the organization for the effective operation of the ISMS.

The extent of documented information can vary depending on 1. the size of the organization and the nature of its activities, processes, products, and services, 2. The complexity of processes and their interactions and 3. The competence of personnel.

Creating & Updating Documentation

When creating and updating documented information, the organization must ensure:

Identification and Description: Proper identification and description, such as a title, date, author, or reference number.
Format and Media: Suitable format (e.g., language, software version, graphics) and media (e.g., paper, electronic).

Review and Approval: Documentation must be reviewed and approved to ensure its suitability and adequacy.

Control of Documents

The organization must control documented information required by the ISMS and ISO 27001 to ensure:

Availability and Suitability: Documentation is available and suitable for use where and when it is needed.

Protection: Adequate protection to prevent loss of confidentiality, improper use, or loss of integrity.

To achieve this, the organization must address the following activities, as applicable:

Distribution, Access, Retrieval, and Use: Controls on how documents are distributed, accessed, retrieved, and used.

Storage and Preservation: Proper storage and preservation of documents, ensuring legibility is maintained.

Control of Changes: Version control and management of changes to documents. ISO 27001 documents are living and evolving documents. During the certification process, the auditor will want to see that it is actively maintained, including any changes made. When done correctly, this contributes to an effective management system. As the version control writer, you must record the version number, date of change, author of the change, and details of the change. Including document approval in your version control is good practice, as it clearly shows when the document was last reviewed and approved, even if no changes were made.

Retention and Disposition: Policies on how long documents should be retained and how they should be disposed of.

Additionally, documented information of external origin, necessary for the planning and operation of the ISMS, must be identified and controlled appropriately.

Note: Access control may involve permissions to view the documentation only or permissions to view and edit the documentation, as necessary.

This clause explains one of the most important components of ISO 27001 and ensures that organizations maintain comprehensive, accurate, and up-to-date documentation to support their ISMS. Proper documentation facilitates effective communication, consistency, and compliance with ISO 27001 requirements. It also ensures that information security practices are transparent, traceable, and continuously improved. Document control processes help protect sensitive information and ensure that all stakeholders have access to the necessary information for their roles within the ISMS.

Clause 8, Operations

Clause 8 of ISO 27001, titled "Operations," outlines the requirements for planning, implementing, and controlling the processes needed to meet the requirements of the ISMS and to execute the actions determined in clause 6. It focuses on the operational aspects of the ISMS, ensuring that all necessary processes are effectively planned, implemented, and controlled by Operational Planning and Control as well as Information Security Risk Management.

This clause covers the following concepts:

Operational Planning & Control

The organization shall:
- **Establish Criteria for the Processes**: Define specific criteria for the processes necessary to meet ISMS requirements.
- **Implement Control of the Processes**: Control these processes according to the established criteria to ensure they are carried out as planned.
- **Documented Information**: Maintain sufficient documented information to ensure confidence that the processes have been executed as intended.

Additionally, the organization shall:

- **Control Planned Changes**: Manage planned changes to processes and review the impact of unintended changes, taking action to mitigate any adverse effects as necessary.
- **Control Externally Provided Processes, Products, or Services**: Ensure that any externally provided processes, products, or services relevant to the ISMS are adequately controlled.

Information Security Risk Assessment

The organization shall:

- **Perform Risk Assessments**: Conduct information security risk assessments at planned intervals or when significant changes are proposed or occur, considering the criteria established in Clause 6.
- **Document Results**: Retain documented information of the results of these risk assessments.

Information Security Risk Treatment

The organization shall:

- **Implement Risk Treatment Plans**: Execute the information security risk treatment plans as determined.
- **Document Results**: Retain documented information of the results of the risk treatment activities.

Clause 9.1, Monitoring & Evaluation

Clause 9.1 of ISO 27001, titled "Monitoring, Measurement, Analysis, and Evaluation," outlines the requirements for systematically tracking and assessing the performance and effectiveness of the information security management system (ISMS). This clause specifies that the organization must:

Determine What to Monitor and Measure: Identify the specific information security processes and controls that need to be monitored and measured.

Select Methods: Choose appropriate methods for monitoring, measurement, analysis, and evaluation to ensure the results are valid. The methods should produce results that are comparable and reproducible.

Define Timing: Establish when monitoring and measuring activities should be performed.

Assign Responsibilities: Specify who is responsible for conducting the monitoring and measuring activities.

Analyze and Evaluate Results: Determine when the results from monitoring and measurement will be analyzed and evaluated.

Assign Analysis Responsibilities: Identify who will analyze and evaluate the monitoring and measurement results.

This is another area of an ISMS where documented information must be maintained per ISO 27001 as evidence of the monitoring, measurement, analysis, and evaluation results.

Clause 9.1 emphasizes the importance of performance evaluation in maintaining a robust and effective ISMS. It ensures that organizations regularly track and assess their information security processes and controls to verify that they are functioning as intended and achieving desired outcomes. Performance evaluation is crucial for several reasons:

- **Continuous Improvement**: Regular monitoring and evaluation help identify areas for improvement, ensuring the ISMS evolves to meet changing threats and organizational needs.
- **Compliance**: Demonstrates compliance with ISO 27001 requirements and other regulatory or contractual obligations.
- **Effectiveness**: Ensures that the implemented security controls are effective in mitigating risks and protecting

information assets.

- **Accountability**: Establishes clear responsibilities and accountability for information security within the organization.
- **Informed Decision-Making**: Provides data-driven insights that support strategic and operational decision-making regarding information security.

Clause 9.2, Internal Audit

Most information security frameworks do not require Internal Audit, but it is one of the most important requirements of ISO 27001. Clause 9.2 of ISO 27001, titled "Internal Audit," outlines the requirements for conducting internal audits to evaluate the effectiveness of the information security management system (ISMS). This clause is divided into two parts: general requirements and the internal audit program.

General Requirements

The organization must conduct internal audits at planned intervals to provide information on whether the ISMS conforms to 1. The organization's own requirements for its ISMS, and 2. The requirements of the ISO 27001 standard. The Internal audits should also be effectively implemented and maintained to ensure that the ISMS is not only compliant but also operating effectively and maintained appropriately.

Internal Audit Program

According to clause 9.2.2 of ISO 27001, the organization must plan, establish, implement, and maintain an internal audit program, which includes:

- **Frequency**: How often audits will be conducted.
- **Methods**: The techniques and procedures used for the audits.
- **Responsibilities**: Who is responsible for conducting

and overseeing the audits.

- **Planning Requirements**: The steps involved in planning the audits.
- **Reporting**: How and to whom the audit results will be reported.

When developing the internal audit program, the organization must consider the importance of the processes being audited as well as the results of previous audits. This is one of the most important items that is forgotten to be implemented by lots of companies that I have seen.

The organization must also:

Define Audit Criteria and Scope: Clearly outline what each audit will cover and the standards it will be measured against.
Select Auditors: Choose auditors who can perform the audits objectively and impartially.

Report Audit Results: Ensure that the findings of the audits are communicated to relevant management.

Documented information must be available as evidence of the implementation of the audit program and the audit results.

Internal audits are a critical component of the ISMS performance evaluation process. They help ensure that the ISMS is functioning as intended and continues to meet both internal and external requirements. It also helps organizations to be fully ready for the external audit aka certification audit.

Clause 9.3, Management Review

Clause 9.3 of ISO 27001, titled "Management Review," details the requirements for top management to periodically review the organization's information security management system (ISMS). This clause ensures that the ISMS remains suitable, adequate, and effective.

General Requirements

Top management must review the organization's ISMS at planned intervals to ensure its ongoing suitability, adequacy, and effectiveness. These intervals can be yearly, quarterly, monthly, or weekly, depending on the organization's needs. ISO 27001 does not specify an explicit requirement regarding the frequency of these reviews. By considering various inputs and making informed decisions, management can ensure that the ISMS adapts to changing circumstances and continues to meet the organization's information security needs.

Management Review Inputs

The management review must consider the following:

Status of Actions from Previous Reviews: Evaluate the progress and effectiveness of actions taken since the last management review.

Changes in External and Internal Issues: Assess changes in external and internal factors that may impact the ISMS.

Changes in Needs and Expectations of Interested Parties: Consider any changes in the requirements and expectations of stakeholders relevant to the ISMS.

Feedback on Information Security Performance by Analyzing Trends in: Nonconformities and corrective actions, monitoring and measurement results, audit results, and fulfillment of information security objectives.

Feedback from Interested Parties: Review feedback from stakeholders regarding the ISMS.

Results of Risk Assessment and Risk Treatment Plan Status: Evaluate the outcomes of recent risk assessments and the current status of the risk treatment plan.

Opportunities for Continual Improvement: Identify potential areas for enhancing the ISMS.

Management Review Results

The results of the management review must include:

- **Decisions on Continual Improvement**: Decisions related to opportunities for continual improvement of the ISMS.
- **Needs for Changes**: Identification of any required changes to the ISMS to improve its performance or adapt to new conditions.

Documented information must be maintained as evidence of the results of the management review.

Clause 10.1, Continual Improvement

This clause emphasizes the need for ongoing efforts to refine and improve the ISMS. While most information security frameworks do not mandate continual improvement, many ISO management systems, such as the Quality Management System in ISO 9001 and the Environmental Management System in ISO 14001, do require continual improvement. Continual improvement involves regularly evaluating the ISMS and making necessary adjustments to address new risks, changes in the organization, and evolving security threats. The goal is to ensure that the ISMS remains effective and aligned with the organization's objectives and external requirements.

During an audit of Clause 10.1, an auditor may request the following types of evidence for achieving continual improvement:

1. **Management Review Minutes**: Records of management reviews that include discussions on the performance of the ISMS and decisions on improvements.
2. **Internal Audit Reports**: Documentation of internal audits that identify areas for improvement and track the implementation of corrective actions.

3. **Risk Assessment Updates**: Evidence of regular risk assessments and updates to the risk treatment plan.
4. **Nonconformity and Corrective Action Records**: Logs of identified nonconformities, root cause analyses, and records of corrective actions taken to address these issues.
5. **Improvement Plans**: Detailed plans outlining specific improvement initiatives, including timelines, responsibilities, and evaluation criteria.
6. **Training and Awareness Programs**: Records of ongoing training and awareness programs aimed at improving information security practices within the organization.
7. **Performance Metrics**: Data and reports showing key performance indicators (KPIs) related to the ISMS, demonstrating improvements over time.
8. **Feedback Mechanisms**: Evidence of feedback from stakeholders, including employees, customers, and partners, and how this feedback is used to drive improvements.

Change Management Records: Documentation of changes made to the ISMS, including rationale, implementation details, and impact assessments.

Clause 10.2, Nonconformities

Clause 10.2 of ISO 27001, titled "Nonconformity and Corrective Action," outlines the steps an organization must take when a nonconformity occurs within the information security management system (ISMS). This clause requires the organization to:

React to the Nonconformity by taking action to control and correct the nonconformity and dealing with the consequences of the nonconformity.

Evaluate the Need for Action to Eliminate Causes by reviewing the nonconformity, determining the causes of the nonconformity, and identifying if similar nonconformities exist or could potentially occur.

Implement Needed Actions: Take the necessary corrective actions to address the nonconformity.

Review Effectiveness: Assess the effectiveness of the corrective actions taken.

Make Necessary Changes: Modify the ISMS if needed to prevent recurrence of the nonconformity.

Corrective actions should be proportionate to the impact of the nonconformities encountered.

The organization must maintain documented information to provide evidence of the nature of the nonconformities and any subsequent actions taken and the results of any corrective actions.

Clause 10.2 ensures that organizations have a systematic approach to identifying, documenting, addressing, and preventing nonconformities within their ISMS. This process is crucial for maintaining the integrity and effectiveness of the ISMS. The key steps involve:

1. **Reaction**: Immediate actions to control and correct the nonconformity and manage its consequences.
2. **Evaluation**: Thorough investigation to understand the root causes of the nonconformity and assess the potential for similar issues.
3. **Implementation**: Execution of corrective actions to address the root causes and prevent recurrence.
4. **Review**: Verification that the corrective actions have effectively resolved the issue.
5. **Modification**: Updating the ISMS as necessary to enhance its robustness and prevent future nonconformities.

During an audit of Clause 10.2, an auditor may request the following types of evidence:

1. **Nonconformity Records**: Logs or records detailing the identified nonconformities, including descriptions and dates.
2. **Corrective Action Plans**: Documents outlining the planned corrective actions, responsible parties, and timelines.
3. **Root Cause Analysis Reports**: Detailed reports of investigations conducted to determine the root causes of nonconformities.
4. **Implementation Records**: Evidence of actions taken to correct nonconformities and address their causes.
5. **Effectiveness Review**: Records of reviews conducted to evaluate the effectiveness of the corrective actions.
6. **ISMS Updates**: Documentation of any changes made to the ISMS as a result of corrective actions, including updated policies and procedures.
7. **Communication Records**: Evidence of communication with relevant stakeholders about the nonconformities and corrective actions.

Bare Minimum Documents for ISO 27001

To achieve ISO 27001:2022 certification, an organization must prepare and maintain several mandatory documents. These documents are essential for demonstrating the implementation and effectiveness of the Information Security Management System (ISMS).

1. **ISMS Scope (Clause 4.3):**
   o Document defining the scope of the ISMS, including boundaries and applicability within the organization.
2. **Information Security Policy (Clause 5.2):**
   o A policy outlining the organization's approach to managing information security and supporting its business objectives.
3. **Risk Assessment and Risk Treatment Methodology (Clause 6.1.2):**
   o Documented methodology for performing risk assessments and determining the treatment of identified risks.
4. **Statement of Applicability (SoA) (Clause 6.1.3):**
   o A document that lists the controls chosen from Annex A, providing justifications for inclusion or exclusion and the status of their implementation.
5. **Risk Assessment Report (Clause 6.1.2):**
   o The results of the risk assessment process, including identified risks and their analysis.
6. **Risk Treatment Plan (Clause 6.1.3):**
   o A plan detailing the actions to manage identified risks, including the selected controls and how they will be implemented.
7. **Information Security Objectives (Clause 6.2):**
   o Documented objectives for information security, aligned with the organization's overall objectives, and a plan for achieving them.
8. **Evidence of Competence (Clause 7.2):**

      o   Records demonstrating that employees and other relevant parties have the necessary competence to fulfill their information security roles.

9. **Documented Information Determined by the Organization as Being Necessary for the Effectiveness of the ISMS (Clause 7.5.1)**:
   - o This can include various procedures, guidelines, and records needed to support the ISMS operations.

10. **Operational Planning and Control (Clause 8.1)**:
    - o Procedures and plans to manage and control the implementation of information security measures.

11. **Results of the Risk Assessments and Risk Treatments (Clause 8.2)**:
    - o Records of the risk assessment and treatment outcomes.

12. **Evidence of the Monitoring and Measurement Results (Clause 9.1)**:
    - o Records showing how the performance of the ISMS and its controls are being monitored and measured.

13. **Internal Audit Program and Results (Clause 9.2)**:
    - o Documentation of the internal audit process, including the program, audit reports, and follow-up actions.

14. **Management Review Results (Clause 9.3)**:
    - o Records of management reviews of the ISMS, including meeting minutes and decisions made.

15. **Nonconformities and Corrective Actions (Clause 10.1)**:
    - o Documentation of nonconformities identified within the ISMS and the corrective actions taken to address them.

Organizations may also maintain additional documents and records to support the effective implementation and management of their ISMS.

Information Security Policy

Writing an information security policy for an organization involves several steps to ensure that it comprehensively covers all aspects of information security, aligns with ISO 27001 requirements, and addresses the specific needs and risks of the organization.

Sample of an Information Security Policy

Introduction

Our organization is committed to ensuring the confidentiality, integrity, and availability of its information assets, in alignment with ISO 27001 standard. This policy provides a framework for managing information security risks and protecting information assets from threats, whether internal or external, deliberate or accidental.

Scope

This policy applies to all employees, contractors, vendors, and any other interested parties with access to the information systems and assets. It covers all information assets, including but not limited to hardware, software, data, and communications infrastructure.

Information Security Objectives

1. **Confidentiality:** Ensure that information is accessible only to those authorized to have access.
2. **Integrity:** Safeguard the accuracy and completeness of information and processing methods.
3. **Availability:** Ensure that authorized users have access to information and associated assets when required.

Information Security Management System (ISMS)

We establish, implement, maintain, and continually improve an Information Security Management System (ISMS) in accordance with the ISO 27001 standard.

Roles and Responsibilities

- **Information Security Manager:** Overall responsibility for the implementation and management of the ISMS.
- **Management:** Support and provide the necessary resources for information security initiatives.
- **Employees:** Follow information security policies and procedures, attend training, and report security incidents.

Risk Management

The information security team will conduct regular risk assessments to identify and evaluate information security risks. Appropriate controls will be implemented to manage and mitigate identified risks to acceptable levels.

Information Security Controls, Measures and Activities

1. **Access Control:**
   o Implement user access management processes to ensure appropriate access rights.
   o Use strong authentication mechanisms and regularly review access rights.
2. **Asset Management:**
   o Maintain an inventory of critical information

assets.

o Classify and handle information according to its sensitivity and criticality.

3. **Physical and Environmental Security:**

o Protect physical assets from threats such as unauthorized access, damage, and theft.

o Implement environmental controls to protect against fire, flood, and other natural disasters.

4. **Communications and Operations Management:**

o Establish operational procedures and responsibilities.

o Ensure secure and reliable operation of information processing facilities.

5. **Information Systems Acquisition, Development, and Maintenance:**

o Ensure that security is an integral part of information systems.

o Apply secure development practices and conduct regular security testing.

6. **Supplier Relationships:**

o Ensure that agreements with suppliers include appropriate security requirements.

o Monitor and review supplier compliance with security requirements.

7. **Information Security Incident Management:**

o Establish procedures for reporting and managing information security incidents.

o Conduct regular incident response training and testing.

8. **Business Continuity Management:**

o Develop and maintain business continuity plans.

o Ensure that critical information assets can be recovered in a timely manner following a disruption.

9. **Compliance:**

o Ensure compliance with relevant legal, regulatory, and contractual requirements.

o Conduct regular internal audits to assess

compliance with the ISMS.
10. **Other Controls:**
    - o Additional controls should be designed and implemented based on the outcomes of the risk management process.
    - o Annex A of ISO 27001 and guidelines in the ISO 27002 standard may be used to select and implement additional controls.

Training and Awareness

All employees will receive regular training and awareness programs to ensure they understand their responsibilities related to information security and are aware of current threats and best practices.

Monitoring and Review

The information security team will monitor and review the performance of the ISMS through regular audits, risk assessments, and management reviews. Continuous improvement will be pursued by addressing non-conformities and implementing corrective actions.

Policy Review

This policy will be reviewed at least annually or when significant changes occur to ensure its continued suitability, adequacy, and effectiveness.

Approval

This policy has been approved on [Date of approval] by [Senior Management/Board of Directors].

Controls

Information Security Control refers to any safeguard or countermeasure put in place to manage and mitigate risks to an organization's information assets. These controls are designed to protect the confidentiality, integrity, and availability of information by preventing, detecting, responding to, or recovering from security incidents. Information security controls have other names as well: Security Control, Control Measure, Safeguard, Countermeasure, and Security Mechanism.

Annex A of ISO 27001:2022 includes 93 information security controls, forming the foundation of an organization's Statement of Applicability (SoA). Compared to the previous version, which had 114 controls, the 2022 update reduced the number of controls. These controls are now categorized into four themes instead of the previous 14 clauses:

1. **Organizational Controls**
2. **People Controls**
3. **Physical Controls**
4. **Technological Controls**

While Annex A provides a framework, the detailed explanations of these controls are available in the ISO 27002:2022 standard. It is important to note that these controls are not mandatory, unlike the clauses 4 to 10 of ISO 27001 which were explained in detail in previous chapters.

As mentioned before, a common misconception is that all Annex A controls must be implemented to achieve ISO 27001 certification. Instead, organizations should use the SoA to specify which controls are relevant based on their risk management processes and management decisions. Only those controls that address the specific needs and risks of the organization should be implemented.

Determining necessary controls requires thorough risk assessment and risk treatment processes. This ensures security measures are tailored to the organization's unique requirements. The goal is to achieve an adequate level of security that addresses business risks, rather than indiscriminately implementing measures to become the most secure organization.

1. Organizational Controls

These controls focus on the administrative and management aspects of information security. They ensure the establishment of a structured and coordinated approach to information security within the organization. We have simplified the language of the controls to make them easier to understand. While these versions are not word-for-word the same as the official ISO 27001 controls, we believe they convey the same meaning and intent. We need not touch the control numbers.

5.1 Policies for Information Security

- **Control**: Information security policies and topic-specific policies must be defined, approved by management, published, communicated to, and acknowledged by relevant personnel and interested parties. These policies should be reviewed at planned intervals or whenever significant changes occur.
- **Possible Evidence:** For this control, auditors may ask for information security policy, other top specific policies for information security, or dissemination of policies to in-scope personnel and/or interested parties.

5.2 Information Security Roles and Responsibilities

- **Control**: Information security roles and responsibilities should be clearly defined and allocated according to the organization's needs.
- **Possible Evidence:** For this control, auditors may ask for allocated roles and responsibilities for the implementation, operation, and management of information security.

5.3 Segregation of Duties

- **Control**: Conflicting duties and areas of responsibility should be segregated to reduce the risk of unauthorized or unintentional modification or misuse of the organization's assets.
- **Possible Evidence:** For this control, auditors may ask for identified conflicting duties or areas of responsibility and established corresponding rules for segregation.

5.4 Management Responsibilities

- **Control**: Management must ensure that all personnel apply information security in accordance with the established information security policy, topic-specific policies, and procedures of the organization.
- **Possible Evidence:** For this control, auditors may ask for management statements and support for information security objectives, policies, procedures, etc. and assignment of personal responsibility for information security to personnel.

5.5 Contact with Authorities

- **Control**: The organization should establish and maintain contact with relevant authorities to facilitate communication during information security incidents.
- **Possible Evidence:** For this control, auditors may ask for defined contact points with relevant authorities, established rules for reporting incidents or defined content for information flow to and from relevant authorities.

5.6 Contact with Special Interest Groups

- **Control**: The organization should establish and maintain contact with special interest groups, specialist security forums, and professional associations to stay informed about security threats and best practices.

- **Possible Evidence:** For this control, auditors may ask for 1. membership and defined contact points with special interest groups, or other forums and associations (e.g., Computer Emergency Response Teams (CERTs), cybersecurity agencies), 2. rules on what can be discussed within such organizations, or 3. defined content for information flow to and from such organizations.

5.7 Threat Intelligence

- **Control:** Information related to information security threats should be collected and analyzed to produce actionable threat intelligence.
- **Possible Evidence:** For this control, auditors may ask for an approach to collecting relevant threat intelligence, or analysis of threat intelligence in relation to the organization and dissemination to appropriate parties.

5.8 Information Security in Project Management

- **Control:** Information security must be integrated into project management to ensure that security controls are considered during the planning and implementation of projects.
- **Possible Evidence:** For this control, auditors may ask for 1. integration of information security in project management throughout the project life cycle, e.g., in requirements definition and testing and 2. for a sample of projects, identified information security risks and corresponding risk treatment.

5.9 Inventory of Information and Other Associated Assets

- **Control:** An inventory of information and other associated assets, including owners, should be developed and maintained.

- **Possible Evidence:** For this control, auditors may ask for maintained inventories of information and other associated assets by the ISMS, maintained ownership of assets in asset inventories, or rules for owner duties for assets, e.g., classification.

5.10 Acceptable Use of Information and Other Associated Assets

- **Control:** Rules for the acceptable use and procedures for handling information and other associated assets should be identified, documented, and implemented.
- **Possible Evidence:** For this control, auditors may ask for documented rules for the acceptable use of information and other associated assets and procedures for handling information and other associated assets.

5.11 Return of Assets

- **Control:** Personnel and other relevant parties must return all organizational assets in their possession upon change or termination of their employment, contract, or agreement.
- **Possible Evidence:** For this control, auditors may ask for 1. rules for the return of the organization's assets, e.g., checklists for change or termination of employment, contract, or agreement, 2. sample of documented return records.

5.12 Classification of Information

- **Control:** Information must be classified according to the organization's information security needs based on confidentiality, integrity, availability, and relevant interested party requirements.
- **Possible Evidence:** For this control, auditors may ask for 1. rules and scheme for the classification of information, e.g., in a topic-specific policy, 2. sample of

information from various sources that should be classified.

5.13 Labeling of Information

- **Control**: An appropriate set of procedures for information labeling must be developed and implemented in accordance with the information classification scheme adopted by the organization.
- **Possible Evidence:** For this control, auditors may ask for 1. rules for labeling information and other associated assets, 2. procedures for labeling specific types of information and other associated assets.

5.14 Information Transfer

- **Control**: Information transfer rules, procedures, or agreements must be in place for all types of transfer facilities within the organization and between the organization and other parties.
- **Possible Evidence:** For this control, auditors may ask for 1. rules for information transfer, such as in a topic-specific policy, 2. definition of use cases for information transfer identified in the ISMS, along with corresponding rules, procedures, or agreements covering physical, electronic, or verbal transfer, 3. samples of implemented information transfer procedures or agreements.

5.15 Access Control

- **Control**: Rules to control physical and logical access to information and other associated assets must be established and implemented based on business and information security requirements.
- **Possible Evidence:** For this control, auditors may ask for 1. rules for controlling physical and logical access to information and other associated assets, such as in a topic-specific access control policy, 2. samples of access rights for high-risk physical or logical access to

information and other assets, checked for conformity to the above rules.

5.16 Identity Management

- **Control**: The full life cycle of identities must be managed.
- **Possible Evidence:** For this control, auditors may ask for procedures for managing identities assigned to persons or non-human entities over their life cycle.

5.17 Authentication Information

- **Control**: Allocation and management of authentication information must be controlled by a management process, including advising personnel on appropriate handling of authentication information.
- **Possible Evidence:** For this control, auditors may ask for 1. description of the process for allocation and management of authentication information, 2. instructions for users on the proper handling of authentication information, 3. security settings for password management systems where passwords are used (e.g., length, complexity, rotation).

5.18 Access Rights

- **Control**: Access rights to information and other associated assets must be provisioned, reviewed, modified, and removed in accordance with the organization's topic-specific policy on and rules for access control.
- **Possible Evidence:** For this control, auditors may ask for 1. rules for access control, such as in a topic-specific access control policy (covering both physical and logical access), 2. description of the process for assigning, updating, or revoking access rights, 3. rules and process for the regular review of access rights, 4. access rights assigned to a sample of identities, 5. results of performed reviews of access rights.

5.19 Information Security in Supplier Relationships

- **Control**: Processes and procedures must be defined and implemented to manage the information security risks associated with the use of suppliers' products or services.
- **Possible Evidence:** For this control, auditors may ask for 1. rules for managing information security risks in supplier relationships, such as in a topic-specific policy on the use of supplier products and services, 2. processes or procedures for managing information security in supplier relationships throughout the life cycle of the relationships, 3. results from supplier evaluations (e.g., ICT infrastructure components, services), 4. results from monitoring conformance to established information security requirements (e.g., for a sample of supplier relationships).

5.20 Addressing Information Security within Supplier Agreements

- **Control**: Relevant information security requirements must be established and agreed upon with each supplier based on the type of supplier relationship.
- **Possible Evidence:** For this control, auditors may ask for 1. register of agreements with external parties related to the type of supplier relationship, 2. sample supplier agreements including relevant information security requirements and Service Level Agreements.

5.21 Managing Information Security in the Information and Communication Technology (ICT) Supply Chain

- **Control**: Processes and procedures must be defined and implemented to manage the information security risks associated with the ICT products and services supply chain.
- **Possible Evidence:** For this control, auditors may ask for 1. rules for handling information security in ICT product or service acquisition. 2. ICT supply chain

information security risk management practices, 3. results of risk analysis performed, including mitigating controls for a sample of specific ICT supply chains.

5.22 Monitoring, Review, and Change Management of Supplier Services

- **Control**: The organization must regularly monitor, review, evaluate, and manage changes in supplier information security practices and service delivery.
- **Possible Evidence:** For this control, auditors may ask for 1. processes for managing changes in supplier information security practices and service delivery, 2. plans for regular monitoring, reviewing, and evaluating supplier information security practices (e.g., through service reports, audits of suppliers), 3. results from monitoring and reviewing activities, including action plans.

5.23 Information Security for Use of Cloud Services

- **Control**: Processes for the acquisition, use, management, and exit from cloud services must be established in accordance with the organization's information security requirements.
- **Possible Evidence:** For this control, auditors may ask for 1. rules for managing information security risks in cloud services, such as in a topic-specific policy on the use of cloud services, 2. list of cloud services used by the organization, 3. processes for managing information security risks associated with the use of cloud services, 4. specific provisions for the protection of the organization's data and availability of services, if the cloud service agreements do not cover the organization's confidentiality, integrity, availability, and information handling requirements.

5.24 Information Security Incident Management Planning and Preparation

- **Control**: The organization must plan and prepare for managing information security incidents by defining, establishing, and communicating information security incident management processes, roles, and responsibilities.
- **Possible Evidence:** For this control, auditors may ask for 1. processes, plans, roles, and responsibilities for handling information security incidents, 2. reporting procedures for information security events, including examples of such reports.

5.25 Assessment and Decision on Information Security Events

- **Control**: The organization must assess information security events and determine if they should be categorized as information security incidents.
- **Possible Evidence:** For this control, auditors may ask for 1. criteria for assessing information security events, 2. categorization and prioritization scheme for information security incidents.

5.26 Response to Information Security Incidents

- **Control**: Information security incidents must be addressed in accordance with documented procedures.
- **Possible Evidence:** For this control, auditors may ask for 1. procedures for information security incident response, 2. records of incidents and corresponding incident responses.

5.27 Learning from Information Security Incidents

- **Control**: Knowledge gained from information security incidents should be used to strengthen and enhance information security controls.

- **Possible Evidence:** For this control, auditors may ask for 1. records of information security incidents that occurred, including types, volumes, and costs incurred, 2. lessons learned from the analysis of information security incidents, including enhancements to the incident management plan, improvement of controls, and awareness activities.

5.28 Collection of Evidence

- **Control:** The organization must establish and implement procedures for the identification, collection, acquisition, and preservation of evidence related to information security events.
- **Possible Evidence:** For this control, auditors may ask for procedures for dealing with evidence related to information security incidents, such as identification, collection, acquisition, and preservation.

5.29 Information Security During Disruption

- **Control:** The organization must plan how to maintain information security at an appropriate level during disruptions.
- **Possible Evidence:** For this control, auditors may ask for 1. plans for maintaining appropriate information security levels during disruptions, 2. inclusion of information security requirements in the business continuity management planning and process.

5.30 ICT Readiness for Business Continuity

- **Control:** ICT readiness must be planned, implemented, maintained, and tested based on business continuity objectives and ICT continuity requirements.
- **Possible Evidence:** For this control, auditors may ask for 1. ICT continuity requirements derived from business impact analysis, 2. ICT continuity plans, 3.

results of regular ICT continuity tests.

5.31 Legal, Statutory, Regulatory, and Contractual Requirements

- **Control**: Legal, statutory, regulatory, and contractual requirements relevant to information security, as well as the organization's approach to meeting these requirements, must be identified, documented, and kept up to date.
- **Possible Evidence:** For this control, auditors may ask for 1. list of relevant countries in which the organization conducts business or uses products and services that can affect the organization's information security, 2. identified external requirements, including legal, regulatory, or contractual requirements relevant to information security, particularly regarding the use of cryptography in any form.

5.32 Intellectual Property Rights

- **Control**: The organization must implement appropriate procedures to protect intellectual property rights.
- **Possible Evidence:** For this control, auditors may ask for 1. rules for managing intellectual property rights, such as in a topic-specific policy, 2. procedures for handling document copyrights, design rights, trademarks, patents, and source code licenses, along with corresponding inventories.

5.33 Protection of Records

- **Control**: Records must be protected from loss, destruction, falsification, unauthorized access, and unauthorized release.
- **Possible Evidence:** For this control, auditors may ask for 1. rules for records management linked to applicable laws, regulations, and contractual requirements, such as in a topic-specific policy, 2. procedures for the storage, handling, chain of custody,

retention, and disposal of records, 3. configuration of data storage systems to meet records management requirements (e.g., preservation, retention).

5.34 Privacy and Protection of Personally Identifiable Information (PII)

- **Control**: The organization must identify and meet requirements for the preservation of privacy and protection of PII in accordance with applicable laws, regulations, and contractual requirements.
- **Possible Evidence:** For this control, auditors may ask for 1. rules for handling personally identifiable information (PII), such as in a topic-specific policy, 2. list of relevant countries in which the organization conducts business or uses products and services that can affect privacy and protection of PII, 3. identified external requirements, including legal, regulatory, or contractual requirements for the preservation of privacy and protection of PII, 4. analyses performed by parties responsible for handling PII to show that requirements are met through appropriate technical and organizational measures.

5.35 Independent Review of Information Security

- **Control**: The organization's approach to managing information security, including people, processes, and technologies, must be reviewed independently at planned intervals or when significant changes occur.
- **Possible Evidence:** For this control, auditors may ask for 1. plans for conducting independent information security reviews, 2. reporting results of the independent reviews (sample) to top management, 3. corrective actions taken when the organization's approach to managing information security is found to be inadequate.

5.36 Compliance with Policies, Rules, and Standards for Information Security

- **Control**: Compliance with the organization's information security policy, topic-specific policies, rules, and standards must be regularly reviewed.
- **Possible Evidence:** For this control, auditors may ask for 1. plans for reviewing the organization's compliance with the information security policy, topic-specific policies, rules, and standards, 2. results of such reviews (sample) and corrective actions taken.

5.37 Documented Operating Procedures

- **Control**: Operating procedures for information processing facilities must be documented and made available to personnel who need them.
- **Possible Evidence:** For this control, auditors may ask for operating procedures for information processing facilities relevant to information security.

2. People Controls

These controls address the human factors in information security, ensuring that personnel are properly screened, trained, and aware of their roles in maintaining information security.

6.1 Screening

- **Control**: Background verification checks on all candidates for employment must be conducted before joining the organization and on an ongoing basis, considering applicable laws, regulations, and ethics. These checks should be proportional to business requirements, the classification of the information to be accessed, and the perceived risks.
- **Possible Evidence:** For this control, auditors may ask for 1. rules and processes for background checks, considering applicable laws, regulations, and ethics, 2.

background checks performed for a sample of new entrants and current personnel as applicable (e.g., promotions, sensitive job profiles).

6.2 Terms and Conditions of Employment

- **Control**: Employment contracts must clearly state the responsibilities of both the personnel and the organization regarding information security.
- **Possible Evidence:** For this control, auditors may ask for 1. general rules or terms and conditions related to information security responsibilities, such as a code of conduct, 2. acceptance of terms and conditions concerning information security by personnel, 3. sample of specific information security responsibilities agreed upon by personnel with critical roles (e.g., access to sensitive information or privileged access to systems).

6.3 Information Security Awareness, Education, and Training

- **Control**: All personnel and relevant interested parties must receive appropriate information security awareness, education, and training. They should also receive regular updates on the organization's information security policies and procedures relevant to their job functions.
- **Possible Evidence:** For this control, auditors may ask for 1. information security awareness, education, and training programs, including specific content for important target groups, 2. attendance list for information security training sessions conducted, 3. responses from interviews with a sample of attendees on expected behaviors.

6.4 Disciplinary Process

- **Control**: A formalized and communicated disciplinary process must be in place to take action against personnel and other relevant interested parties who violate information security policies.

- **Possible Evidence:** For this control, auditors may ask for formal disciplinary process, as communicated to personnel and other relevant interested parties.

6.5 Responsibilities After Termination or Change of Employment

- **Control**: Information security responsibilities and duties that remain valid after the termination or change of employment must be clearly defined, enforced, and communicated to relevant personnel and interested parties.
- **Possible Evidence:** For this control, auditors may ask for signed acceptance by personnel of specific responsibilities and duties valid after leaving the company or changing employment.

6.6 Confidentiality or Non-disclosure Agreements

- **Control**: Confidentiality or non-disclosure agreements, reflecting the organization's need to protect information, must be identified, documented, regularly reviewed, and signed by personnel and relevant interested parties.
- **Possible Evidence:** For this control, auditors may ask for signed confidentiality agreements by personnel and other relevant interested parties.

6.7 Remote Working

- **Control**: Security measures must be implemented to protect information accessed, processed, or stored outside the organization's premises when personnel are working remotely.
- **Possible Evidence:** For this control, auditors may ask for 1. rules on working remotely, such as in a topic-specific policy, 2. samples of physical and

communication security measures, 3. design of secure information processing devices permitted for remote use (e.g., 'Bring your own device' (BYOD), laptops).

6.8 Information Security Event Reporting

- **Control**: The organization must provide mechanisms for personnel to report observed or suspected information security events through appropriate channels in a timely manner.
- **Possible Evidence:** For this control, auditors may ask for 1. mechanism for reporting information security events that can be identified by personnel, 2. instructions or communications to raise awareness on the reporting of information security events.

3. Physical Controls

These controls focus on the physical protection of information assets, ensuring that secure areas and environmental safeguards are in place to protect against physical threats.

7.1 Physical Security Perimeters

- **Control:** Security perimeters must be defined and used to protect areas containing information and associated assets.
- **Possible Evidence:** For this control, auditors may ask for 1. rules for constructing secure areas and the strength of physical barriers, 2. physical security perimeter and secure area design for each relevant location.

7.2 Physical Entry

- **Control:** Secure areas must be protected by appropriate entry controls and access points.
- **Possible Evidence:** For this control, auditors may ask for 1. access authorization system (physical or

electronic) for entry points to secure areas, 2. logs tracking access of personnel and visitors, 3. physical design of delivery and loading areas with corresponding process descriptions.

7.3 Securing Offices, Rooms, and Facilities

- **Control:** Physical security measures for offices, rooms, and facilities must be designed and implemented.
- **Possible Evidence:** For this control, auditors may ask for physical security design and implementation of offices and facilities for shielding sensitive information being processed.

7.4 Physical Security Monitoring

- **Control:** Premises must be continuously monitored for unauthorized physical access.
- **Possible Evidence:** For this control, auditors may ask for 1. design of physical surveillance systems to detect unauthorized physical access, 2. protection measures for monitoring systems, 3. logs generated by the operation of physical surveillance systems.

7.5 Protecting Against Physical and Environmental Threats

- **Control**: Design and implement protections against physical and environmental threats, such as natural disasters and other intentional or unintentional physical threats to infrastructure.
- **Possible Evidence:** For this control, auditors may ask for 1. outcome of risk assessments on physical and environmental threats, 2. design of appropriate measures to protect against physical and environmental threats.

7.6 Working in Secure Areas

- **Control**: Design and implement security measures for working in secure areas.

- **Possible Evidence:** For this control, auditors may ask for 1. rules for working in secure areas, specifying specific security measures, 2. implemented security measures for secure areas.

7.7 Clear Desk and Clear Screen

- **Control**: Define and appropriately enforce clear desk rules for papers and removable storage media, as well as clear screen rules for information processing facilities.
- **Possible Evidence:** For this control, auditors may ask for 1. rules for clear desk and clear screen policies, such as in a topic-specific policy, 2. spot checks on clear desk and clear screen behaviors (e.g., work areas and printers).

7.8 Equipment Siting and Protection

- **Control**: Ensure that equipment is securely sited and protected.
- **Possible Evidence:** For this control, auditors may ask for 1. rules for equipment siting and protection, 2. spot checks on equipment siting and protection.

7.9 Security of Assets Off-Premises

- **Control**: Protect assets that are used or stored off-site.
- **Possible Evidence:** For this control, auditors may ask for 1. rules for the use of assets outside the organization's premises (e.g., BYOD guidelines), results of interviews or surveys performed among personnel using assets outside the organization's premises.

7.10 Storage Media

- **Control**: Manage storage media through their entire life cycle of acquisition, use, transportation, and disposal in accordance with the organization's classification scheme and handling requirements.

- **Possible Evidence:** For this control, auditors may ask for 1. rules for the use of removable storage media, such as in a topic-specific policy, 2. device configurations to restrict or protect the transfer of information to and from removable storage media (e.g., encryption), 3. processes for secure disposal of assets and records from such processes.

7.11 Supporting Utilities

- **Control**: Protect information processing facilities from power failures and other disruptions caused by failures in supporting utilities.
- **Possible Evidence:** For this control, auditors may ask for 1. installed utility protection measures, especially in data centers (e.g., temperature, electric supply, water), 2. emergency provisions to cut off power, water, gas, or other utilities.

7.12 Cabling Security

- **Control**: Protect cables carrying power, data, or supporting information services from interception, interference, or damage.
- **Possible Evidence:** For this control, auditors may ask for the physical routing and protection of cabling.

7.13 Equipment Maintenance

- **Control**: Maintain equipment correctly to ensure the availability, integrity, and confidentiality of information.
- **Possible Evidence:** For this control, auditors may ask for 1. procedures for the maintenance of different types of equipment, 2. equipment maintenance records.

7.14 Secure Disposal or Reuse of Equipment

- **Control**: Verify that any sensitive data and licensed software have been removed or securely overwritten before disposing of or reusing equipment containing storage media.
- **Possible Evidence:** For this control, auditors may ask for 1. rules for the disposal or reuse of equipment containing storage media, 2. records of physical or logical destruction of information or equipment.

4. Technological Controls

These controls involve the use of technology to protect information. They cover various aspects of information security, including network security, encryption, and application security.

8.1 User Endpoint Devices

- **Control:** Protect information stored on, processed by, or accessible via user endpoint devices.
- **Possible Evidence:** For this control, auditors may ask for 1. rules on the secure configuration and handling of user endpoint devices, such as in a topic-specific policy, 2. end-user awareness activities covering security requirements and procedures for protecting user endpoint devices, 3. rules on the separation and protection of business information on private devices (BYOD), if applicable, 4. design of secure information processing devices permitted for remote use (e.g., BYOD, laptops).

8.2 Privileged Access Rights

- **Control:** Restrict and manage the allocation and use of privileged access rights.
- **Possible Evidence:** For this control, auditors may ask for 1. rules on the restricted allocation, use, and monitoring of privileged access rights, such as in a

topic-specific policy, 2. authorization and review processes to manage privileged access rights.

8.3 Information Access Restriction

- **Control:** Restrict access to information and other associated assets in accordance with the established access control policy.
- **Possible Evidence:** For this control, auditors may ask for 1. rules on the restrictions of access to information and other associated assets, such as in a topic-specific policy, 2. access management techniques and processes to protect access to sensitive information throughout its life cycle (i.e., creation, processing, storage, transmission, disposal).

8.4 Access to Source Code

- **Control:** Appropriately manage read and write access to source code, development tools, and software libraries.
- **Possible Evidence:** For this control, auditors may ask for the procedures for managing read and write access to source code, development tools, and software libraries.

8.5 Secure Authentication

- **Control**: Implement secure authentication technologies and procedures based on information access restrictions and the organization's access control policy.
- **Possible Evidence:** For this control, auditors may ask for 1. rules on authentication technologies and procedures for access control, such as in a topic-specific policy, 2. risk-based decisions and corresponding implementations of log-on procedures for systems or applications, 3. use of strong or multi-factor authentication for critical information systems.

8.6 Capacity Management

- **Control**: Monitor and adjust the use of resources to meet current and expected capacity requirements.
- **Possible Evidence:** For this control, auditors may ask for 1. current and expected capacity requirements, 2. measurements of resource usage, such as information processing facilities, human resources, offices, and other facilities, 3. procedures for either providing sufficient capacity or reducing capacity requirements.

8.7 Protection Against Malware

- **Control**: Implement protection against malware and support it with appropriate user awareness training.
- **Possible Evidence:** For this control, auditors may ask for 1. rules for protection against malware, 2. risk-based coverage of assets and corresponding configuration of malware detection software, 3. other procedures and measures to protect information and other resources against malware, 4. end-user awareness activities regarding malware.

8.8 Management of Technical Vulnerabilities

- **Control**: Obtain information about technical vulnerabilities in use, evaluate the organization's exposure to such vulnerabilities, and take appropriate measures to address them.
- **Possible Evidence:** For this control, auditors may ask for 1. collection and management of information about technical vulnerabilities in information systems in use, 2. results of vulnerability scans (regularly performed) or from penetration tests, 3. evaluations of the organization's exposure to technical vulnerabilities and planned mitigating measures, 4. software update process to ensure the installation of the most up-to-date approved patches and application updates.

8.9 Configuration Management

- **Control**: Establish, document, implement, monitor, and review configurations, including security configurations, of hardware, software, services, and networks.
- **Possible Evidence:** For this control, auditors may ask for 1. rules on configurations, including security configurations, of hardware, software, services, and networks, 2. processes for managing, implementing, applying, monitoring, and reviewing configurations, 3. standard templates for the secure configuration of hardware, software, services, and networks (i.e., hardening).

8.10 Information Deletion

- **Control**: Delete information stored in information systems, devices, or any other storage media when it is no longer required.
- **Possible Evidence:** For this control, auditors may ask for 1. rules for the timely deletion of information stored in information systems, devices, or any other storage media, such as in a topic-specific data retention policy, 2. procedures for securely deleting sensitive information on systems, applications, and services, 3. third-party agreements with provisions for information deletion where third parties store the organization's information.

8.11 Data Masking

- **Control**: Use data masking in accordance with the organization's access control policy and other related policies, considering business requirements and applicable legislation.
- **Possible Evidence:** For this control, auditors may ask for 1. rules on data masking, such as in the organization's topic-specific access control policy, 2. results of analyses performed to determine where the protection of sensitive information (e.g., PII) requires

techniques such as data masking, pseudonymization, or anonymization, 3. techniques used for data masking, pseudonymization, or anonymization.

8.12 Data Leakage Prevention

- **Control**: Apply data leakage prevention measures to systems, networks, and any other devices that process, store, or transmit sensitive information.
- **Possible Evidence:** For this control, auditors may ask for 1. rules on data leakage prevention measures to be applied to systems, networks, and any other devices that process, store, or transmit sensitive information, 2. identified information requiring protection against leakage, 3. identified relevant leakage channels with measures to prevent leakage, including monitoring, 4. configuration of data loss prevention systems.

8.13 Information Backup

- **Control**: Maintain and regularly test backup copies of information, software, and systems in accordance with the agreed backup policy.
- **Possible Evidence:** For this control, auditors may ask for 1. rules on the backup of information, software, and systems, such as in a topic-specific backup policy, 2. backup plans based on the established business requirements of the organization, 3. operational procedures for monitoring the timely and correct execution of backups and addressing failures, 4. backup restoration tests performed at regular intervals.

8.14 Redundancy of Information Processing Facilities

- **Control**: Implement redundancy in information processing facilities to meet availability requirements.
- **Possible Evidence:** For this control, auditors may ask for 1. identified requirements for the availability of business services and information systems, 2.

architecture of systems with high availability requirements, providing appropriate redundancy, 3. results of failover tests performed.

8.15 Logging

- **Control**: Produce, store, protect, and analyze logs that record activities, exceptions, faults, and other relevant events.
- **Possible Evidence:** For this control, auditors may ask for 1. rules on the purpose of log creation, data collection, and specific requirements for handling log data, such as in a topic-specific logging policy, 2. list of security-relevant logs and measures to ensure their protection against unauthorized manipulations, 3. procedures for performing regular analysis and interpretation of log events to identify unusual activities or anomalous behavior, 4. configuration of log systems.

8.16 Monitoring Activities

- **Control**: Monitor networks, systems, and applications for anomalous behavior and take appropriate actions to evaluate potential information security incidents.
- **Possible Evidence:** For this control, auditors may ask for 1. rules for monitoring networks, systems, and applications for anomalous behavior, 2. established baselines of normal behavior and criteria for triggering alerts, 3. monitoring logs maintained for defined retention periods, 4. results of analyses performed to identify anomalous behavior.

8.17 Clock Synchronization

- **Control**: Synchronize the clocks of information processing systems with approved time sources.
- **Possible Evidence:** For this control, auditors may ask for 1. list of reference time sources used by the organization, 2. clock synchronization methods and

handling of time differences.

8.18 Use of Privileged Utility Programs

- **Control**: Restrict and tightly control the use of utility programs that can override system and application controls.
- **Possible Evidence:** For this control, auditors may ask for 1. list of utility programs that may be capable of overriding system and application controls, 2. processes, procedures, and other methods used to restrict and tightly control such utility programs.

8.19 Installation of Software on Operational Systems

- **Control**: Implement procedures and measures to securely manage software installation on operational systems.
- **Possible Evidence:** For this control, auditors may ask for 1. procedures and measures for managing the installation of software on operational systems, including inventories of installed software with versions, 2. rules on which types of software users are allowed to install, 3. restrictions on installing software by persons other than trained administrators.

8.20 Network Security

- **Control**: Secure, manage, and control networks and network devices to protect information in systems and applications.
- **Possible Evidence:** For this control, auditors may ask for 1. rules for ensuring the security of information in networks and protecting connected services from unauthorized access, 2. measures and security features implemented to protect information in networks and supporting information processing facilities, such as configuration templates, configuration of cryptographic controls, rule sets of gateways, and sample configurations of network devices, 3. network

architecture documentation, including diagrams, configuration files, and segregation, 4. rules for authenticating system connections to the network.

8.21 Security of Network Services

- **Control**: Identify, implement, and monitor security mechanisms, service levels, and requirements of network services.
- **Possible Evidence:** For this control, auditors may ask for 1. rules on the secure use of networks and network services, 2. list of networks and network services used, along with security mechanisms and service levels, 3. assurance obtained from network service providers.

8.22 Segregation of Networks

- **Control**: Segregate groups of information services, users, and information systems within the organization's networks.
- **Possible Evidence:** For this control, auditors may ask for 1. rules on segregation of network domains based on levels of trust, criticality, and sensitivity, according to the topic-specific policy on access control, 2. network topology (including wireless) and segregation of zones with descriptions of purpose and rules, 3. definitions of security perimeters for network domains, 4. processes to manage security perimeters of network domains, including firewall rules.

8.23 Web Filtering

- **Control**: Manage access to external websites to reduce exposure to malicious content.
- **Possible Evidence:** For this control, auditors may ask for 1. rules on the safe and appropriate use of online resources, including any restrictions on undesirable or inappropriate websites, 2. measures implemented to reduce exposure to malicious content from external websites, such as filtering rules, 3. awareness and

training activities delivered to all personnel on the secure and appropriate use of online resources.

8.24 Use of Cryptography

- **Control**: Define and implement rules for the effective use of cryptography, including cryptographic key management.
- **Possible Evidence:** For this control, auditors may ask for 1. rules for the effective use of cryptography, including acceptable ciphers and key management, as outlined in a topic-specific policy on cryptography, 2. list of cryptographic techniques used by the organization, 3. standards, procedures, and methods for key management, including generating, storing, archiving, retrieving, distributing, retiring, and destroying cryptographic keys.

8.25 Secure Development Life Cycle

- **Control**: Establish and apply rules for the secure development of software and systems.
- **Possible Evidence:** For this control, auditors may ask for 1. rules on secure software development to ensure information security is integrated into the secure development life cycle, 2. separation between development, test, and production environments, 3. security processes and checkpoints to ensure adequate coverage of information security requirements throughout the entire software development life cycle, 4. assurance obtained for the appropriate handling of information security requirements when software development is outsourced.

8.26 Application Security Requirements

- **Control**: Identify, specify, and approve information security requirements when developing or acquiring applications.
- **Possible Evidence:** For this control, auditors may ask

for 1. process for defining application security requirements based on specific risk assessments, 2. application risk assessments performed, detailing specific information security requirements, 3. requirements identified for a sample of recent application developments/implementations, particularly for transactional services, electronic ordering, and payment applications.

8.27 Secure System Architecture and Engineering Principles

- **Control**: Establish, document, maintain, and apply principles for engineering secure systems in all information system development activities.
- **Possible Evidence:** For this control, auditors may ask for 1. architecture and security engineering principles established to ensure that information systems are securely designed, implemented, and operated within the development life cycle, 2. integration of security engineering principles into software development, 3. sample application-specific security implementations confirming the use of the above engineering principles, 4. embedded secure engineering principles in contracts for outsourced development, if applicable.

8.28 Secure Coding

- **Control**: Apply secure coding principles to software development.
- **Possible Evidence:** For this control, auditors may ask for 1. rules on secure coding principles used for both new developments and in reuse scenarios, 2. Processes for ensuring the application of secure coding principles during planning and pre-coding, during coding, and during review and maintenance, 3. Application of specific secure coding principles in recent development activities, including the use of code scanning techniques, 4. Protection mechanisms for code, including access restrictions.

8.29 Security Testing in Development and Acceptance

- **Control**: Define and implement security testing processes throughout the development life cycle.
- **Possible Evidence:** For this control, auditors may ask for 1. rules on security testing to validate that information security requirements are met when applications or code are deployed to the production environment, 2. samples of sets of requirements actually used for security testing, along with corresponding test results, 3. output and follow-up from automated test tools (e.g., code analysis tools, vulnerability scanners, functional tests).

8.30 Outsourced Development

- **Control**: Direct, monitor, and review activities related to outsourced system development.
- **Possible Evidence:** For this control, auditors may ask for 1. rules on how information security measures required by the organization should be implemented in outsourced system development, 2. procedures implemented to direct, monitor, and review activities related to outsourced system development, 3. outcome of monitoring or reviewing suppliers to ensure expectations are met.

8.31 Separation of Development, Test, and Production Environments

- **Control**: Separate and secure development, testing, and production environments.
- **Possible Evidence:** For this control, auditors may ask for 1. rules for the level of separation between production, testing, and development environments, including specific requirements for different development environments, 2. separation between development, test, and production environments, 3. protection measures for test and production environments (e.g., access restrictions, network

segregation, ensuring no sensitive production information is used).

8.32 Change Management

- **Control**: Subject changes to information processing facilities and information systems to change management procedures.
- **Possible Evidence:** For this control, auditors may ask for 1. rules for managing changes to preserve information security, 2. change control procedures, including documentation, specification, testing, quality control, and managed implementation, 3. sample of changes performed, showing how changes were tested, approved, and deployed.

8.33 Test Information

- **Control**: Appropriately select, protect, and manage test information.
- **Possible Evidence:** For this control, auditors may ask for 1. rules for the appropriate selection, use, protection, and management of test information, 2. procedures for protecting operational information during its use for testing purposes (e.g., masking), 3. samples of information deletion from test environments.

8.34 Protection of information systems during audit testing

- **Control**: Audit tests and other assurance activities involving assessment of operational systems shall be planned and agreed between the tester and appropriate management.
- **Possible Evidence:** For this control, auditors may ask for 1. list of requests for audit tests or other assurance activities involving the assessment of operational systems, 2. sample of performed audit tests and how these were agreed upon and conducted.

ISMS Implementation

Implementing an Information Security Management System (ISMS) based on ISO 27001 involves a systematic approach. Implementing an Information Security Management System (ISMS) based on ISO 27001 requires a systematic approach. To familiarize yourself with best practices for implementing an ISMS according to ISO 27001 requirements, refer to ISO 27003. Here are some recommended steps to get started:

Step 1: Obtain Management Support

- Present a business case highlighting the benefits of ISO 27001 implementation, such as improved security posture, compliance with legal requirements, and enhanced customer trust.
- Ensure top management commits to the necessary resources, including budget, personnel, and time.

Step 2: Define the Scope

- Clearly outline the areas, processes, and systems included in the ISMS scope.
- Consider factors such as organizational structure, geographical locations, and the types of information processed.

Step 3: Conduct a Risk Assessment

- Establish a risk assessment framework that includes risk identification, risk analysis, and risk evaluation.
- Use tools and techniques such as interviews, questionnaires, and vulnerability assessments to identify risks.
- Prioritize risks based on their likelihood and potential impact on the organization.

Step 4: Develop an ISMS Policy

- Create a policy document that reflects the organization's commitment to information security.
- Ensure the policy is approved by top management and communicated to all relevant stakeholders.

Step 5: Set ISMS Objectives

- Align objectives with the organization's strategic goals and the ISMS policy.
- Ensure objectives are specific, measurable, achievable, relevant, and time bound.

Step 6: Identify and Implement Controls

- Select controls from Annex A of ISO 27001 and other relevant security frameworks like NIST 800-53 based on the risk assessment.
- Document the rationale for selecting or excluding controls in the Statement of Applicability (SoA).

Step 7: Develop Required Documentation

- Create documents such as risk treatment plans, security policies, procedures, and guidelines.
- Ensure documentation is accessible to relevant personnel and regularly reviewed and updated.

Step 8: Implement the Controls and ISMS

- Integrate security controls into business processes and systems.
- Conduct training sessions to ensure staff understand and comply with security policies and procedures.
- Promote a culture of security awareness and responsibility throughout the organization.

Step 9: Conduct Internal Audits

- Develop an internal audit plan and schedule regular audits to evaluate the ISMS's effectiveness.
- Ensure auditors are independent and competent to provide an objective assessment.
- Document audit findings and take corrective actions to address any non-conformities.

Step 10: Review and Improve the ISMS

- Conduct regular management reviews to assess the ISMS's performance and identify areas for improvement.
- Use data from audits, incidents, and feedback to drive continual improvement.
- Update the risk assessment and control measures as needed to address new or evolving threats.

Step 11: Prepare for Certification

- Engage an accredited certification body to conduct an external audit.
- Ensure all ISMS documentation is up-to-date and accessible to auditors.
- Address any findings from the external audit to achieve ISO 27001 certification.

Recommendations for ISO 27001 Implementation

Utilize Existing Technologies

Begin by designing the system using the technology already in place within the organization. Most organizations have the necessary tools and infrastructure for implementing an Information Security Management System (ISMS). This approach reduces initial complexity and leverages familiar technologies. During the continual improvement phase, the system can be optimized with more efficient technologies, ensuring a smoother transition and minimizing disruption.

Integrate ISMS into Existing Processes

Adjust current customized processes to meet the requirements of the ISMS framework. This ensures that the ISMS is seamlessly incorporated into the organization's operational workflow. It is crucial to avoid creating processes that do not align with the organization's culture, as this can lead to resistance and implementation challenges. Integration should be smooth and coherent with existing practices to facilitate acceptance and adherence.

Apply Continual Improvement Principles

Embrace the principles of continual improvement by actively considering and incorporating feedback and suggestions from interested parties. Set achievable, minor goals at the project's outset and target progressive improvement over the long term. This approach fosters a culture of ongoing enhancement and adaptability, ensuring the ISMS evolves and improves in response to changing needs and challenges.

Engage Interested Parties

Early in the implementation process, clearly define the roles and responsibilities of all interested parties. Ensure their involvement is secured and their support is maintained throughout the project. This engagement is essential for fostering a collaborative environment and ensuring that the ISMS is comprehensive and effective, addressing the concerns and requirements of all stakeholders.

Secure Management Support

Obtain explicit support from management to ensure they understand the project's significance and are committed to its success. Management's role is crucial in providing the necessary resources, such as funding, personnel, and tools. Additionally, they are responsible for performing regular reviews of the management system to ensure ongoing compliance and effectiveness. Their active involvement is key to sustaining the ISMS.

Appoint an ISMS Project Manager

Identify and formally appoint a project manager dedicated to the ISMS implementation. This individual will be responsible for overseeing the entire process, ensuring that operations run smoothly and that the project adheres to timelines and budgets. The project manager will coordinate approvals, manage resources, and serve as the central point of contact, facilitating communication and resolving issues promptly. This role is critical for the successful implementation and maintenance of the ISMS.

Myths and Misconceptions

- A common misconception is that ISO 27001 certifications are issued directly by the International Organization for Standardization (ISO). In reality, ISO itself does not issue certifications. Instead, certifications are granted by independent organizations known as Certification Bodies (CBs), which are accredited by Accreditation Bodies (ABs). The International Organization for Standardization (ISO) develops and publishes international standards, including ISO 27001. However, ISO does not engage in the certification process itself. Its primary role is to provide the framework and guidelines that organizations can follow to establish, implement, and maintain an effective Information Security Management System (ISMS). Certification Bodies are independent organizations that conduct audits and assessments to determine whether an organization's ISMS complies with the requirements of ISO 27001. These CBs are hired by organizations for auditing and issuing ISO 27001 certificates. Certification Bodies issue the ISO 27001 certification if their audit meets the standard's criteria. Again, it is important to note that Certification Bodies operate independently of ISO. There is no direct or indirect connection or affiliation between ISO and the organizations that issue ISO 27001 certifications. The role of ISO ends at the creation and publication of the standard.

- It is a myth that you can implement an ISO 27001 ISMS effectively without senior management commitment. While it is technically possible, it is not recommended and is likely to be less effective. Senior management commitment is crucial because it sets the tone for the entire organization and ensures support through the allocation of resources and funding. Without senior management backing, employees are less likely to recognize the importance of information security and comply with ISMS policies and procedures.

Additionally, obtaining the necessary resources and budget to implement effective security controls and technologies becomes challenging without senior management support. Ultimately, the absence of senior management commitment leads to a fragmented and poorly managed security program, which fails to adequately mitigate or prevent key risks and threats.

- It is a myth that ISO auditors are always knowledgeable experts. They may not necessarily be security or privacy subject matter experts and might not fully understand every aspect of ISO 27001. As a result, they can sometimes misinterpret the standard. When in doubt, refer to ISO 27000, ISO 27001, and ISO 27002, as these are the definitive sources. In my experience, I have encountered auditors who requested items not mandated by ISO 27001. For instance, one auditor insisted on a Business Impact Analysis (BIA) despite it not being a requirement of ISO 27001. He argued that BIA is essential for any Business Continuity Plan (BCP) and, since BCP is a requirement for ISO 27001, BIA documents must be provided as well. While it is true that a BIA is beneficial for creating a robust BCP, ISO 27001 does not specifically mandate it. The auditor justified his request by stating that he had always asked for a BIA in his audits, and all previous auditees had provided it! Although having a BIA is a best practice for designing an effective BCP, it is important to remember that ISO 27001 itself does not explicitly require it. Always cross-check auditor requests against the actual standards to ensure compliance and avoid unnecessary documentation. I've experienced similar issues during PCI-DSS and other audits. Auditors have requested documentation or controls not explicitly required by the standards, frameworks or regulations. This highlights the importance of cross-referencing audit requests with the actual standards to ensure compliance and avoid unnecessary efforts.

- It is a myth that all security controls in Annex A of the

ISO 27001 standard must be implemented to achieve certification. The Statement of Applicability (SoA) specifies which controls should be implemented. However, excluding any of the requirements specified in clauses 4 to 10 is not acceptable if an organization claims conformity to ISO 27001. In other words, you need to implement only those security controls that are necessary for your business needs. Determining which controls are required involves a thorough analysis, which can be time-consuming. Remember, the goal is not to become the most secure organization in the world or to implement security measures for their own sake. Risk assessment and risk treatment processes help determine the appropriate security measures for your business.

- It is a myth that you cannot modify the language of a control or implement a revised version of a control for ISO 27001 certification. For example, Cisco developed the Cisco Cloud Controls Framework (CCF) for ISO 27001, which is available at https://www.cisco.com/c/en/us/about/trust-center/compliance/ccf.html. The Cisco CCF is a rationalized framework that integrates comprehensive controls from various security compliance frameworks and standards. It offers a "build-once-use-many" approach, facilitating multiple certifications such as ISO 27001, ISO 27017, ISO 27018, ISO 27701, ISO 22301, and more. The Cisco CCF does not include the exact controls listed in Annex A of ISO 27001, but you can implement these alternative controls and request an auditor to assess your compliance with ISO 27001. Similarly, you can design your own set of security controls to maintain an ISMS, provided they are based on the guidelines of the ISO 27001 standard and align with your risk management processes.

- It is a myth that ISO is a regulation. ISO 27001 is not mandated by any governmental authority. Instead, it is an international standard developed by the

International Organization for Standardization (ISO) and the International Electrotechnical Commission (IEC). ISO 27001 provides a framework for establishing, implementing, maintaining, and continually improving an Information Security Management System (ISMS). As you know, organizations adopt ISO 27001 voluntarily to enhance their information security practices, demonstrate their commitment to protecting sensitive data, and gain a competitive advantage. However, compliance with ISO 27001 or similar standards may be required by certain industries or sectors as part of contractual obligations or regulatory requirements set by industry bodies. These are not direct government mandates. For instance, a government body like the Committee on Foreign Investment in the United States (CFIUS) might require compliance with ISO 27001 in a contract. I worked for a company that had to comply with ISO 27001 due to such a contractual requirement from CFIUS

- It is a myth that the ISO 27001 standard contains very detailed and comprehensive technical requirements. For example, someone with limited understanding of ISO 27001 might claim that the standard requires passwords to be at least 12 characters long or mandates vulnerability scans every quarter. This is not true. ISO 27001 does not specify such details. Unfortunately, this type of misinformation is common. People who make these claims likely have never read the standard. Please keep in mind that ISO 27001 is designed to be adaptable for all kinds of organizations, from small nonprofits to large multinational corporations. As such, not all requirements are applicable to every type of organization. The standard provides a framework for establishing, implementing, maintaining, and continually improving an Information Security Management System (ISMS), but it allows organizations the flexibility to determine the specific controls and practices that best meet their needs based on a risk assessment.

- It is a myth that ISO 27001 focuses solely on digital assets and IT systems. Implementing a robust information security program involves all departments and all aspects of the business, including IT, operations, human resources, product management, manufacturing, supply chain, marketing, sales, legal, and other business areas. The most important rule is to ensure that information security is integrated throughout the entire organization, addressing every component that contributes to its overall security posture.

- It is a myth that ISO 27001 can be implemented in a month or two. While it is possible to quickly establish an ISO 27001 compliant ISMS and pass the audit, such an approach is unlikely to be effective. The result would be a set of documented policies and procedures that no one in your organization actually follows or values. Proper implementation requires thorough integration into the organizational culture, which takes time, effort and commitment.

- It is a myth that ISO 27001 is all about documentation. Although documentation is a very important part of an ISMS implementation, it is not sufficient. The ultimate goal is performing activities in a safe and secure way, and the documentation is just another tool to help you to achieve that goal. Moreover, the records you produced would become a measure to help you check whether or not you have achieved your goals and enable you to correct those activities that failed or stopped being successful.

- It is a myth that the only benefit of ISO 27001 is for marketing purposes. You might hear statements like, "We are doing this just to get the certificate to show our partners and customers." While ISO 27001 certification does have significant promotional and sales advantages, it also offers numerous other benefits as outlined in chapter one of this book. These include improving your information security posture, enhancing risk management, and fostering a culture of continuous improvement within your organization.

- It's a myth that a section for privacy has been added to ISO 27001:2022. The new title of the standard, "Information security, cybersecurity and privacy protection — Information security management systems — Requirements," might be misleading. The previous title was "Information technology — Security techniques — Information security management systems — Requirements." Despite the new title, no new privacy sections have been added. Don't judge a book by its cover! Privacy is specifically addressed in two separate extensions of ISO 27001: ISO 27018 and ISO 27701, which are individual standards focused on privacy.

- It is a myth that once you achieve ISO 27001 certification, you don't need to do anything for the next three years. While the certification is typically valid for three years, maintaining it requires annual surveillance audits by the ISO 27001 auditor. These audits ensure that the Information Security Management System (ISMS) continues to meet ISO 27001 standards and is effectively maintained throughout the certification period.

- It is a myth that you must have someone within your organization to conduct an ISO 27001 internal audit. If you lack a qualified individual or the necessary competence internally, you can outsource this task to an external professional or company. However, if you plan to use an internal resource for conducting the ISO 27001 internal audit, it is essential to avoid any conflict of interest. This means that the person who designed or implemented any part of the ISMS cannot serve as the internal auditor for ISO 27001.

Some Myths about ISO 27001 Annex A Controls

- It is a myth that a BIA is required. While a Business Impact Analysis (BIA) is a best practice for designing an effective Business Continuity Plan (BCP), ISO 27001 itself does not explicitly require it, neither in Annex A nor elsewhere. Control 5.30 of ISO 27001:2022, which pertains to Business Continuity, does not mandate a BIA. Instead, it states: "ICT readiness shall be planned, implemented, maintained and tested based on business continuity objectives and ICT continuity requirements." This means that while ICT continuity should align with business continuity goals, a formal or separate BIA document is not specifically demanded by the ISO 27001:2022 standard. However, if you take a look at ISO 27002:2022, you can see it states that "The ICT continuity requirements are the outcome of the business impact analysis (BIA)."!

- It is a myth that ISO 27001's Business Continuity control must cover all functions, departments, and business units within an organization. Remember, ISO 27001 focuses specifically on Information Security, not the entire business. Control 5.30 of ISO 27001 addresses ICT readiness for business continuity, not the entire organization. According to Control 5.30, "ICT readiness shall be planned, implemented, maintained and tested based on business continuity objectives and ICT continuity requirements." This means the control is concerned with ensuring the continuity of ICT systems in support of business objectives, rather than encompassing the entire organizational scope.

- It is a myth that ISO 27001:2022 added a requirement for a Web Application Firewall (WAF). This misconception arises from a misunderstanding of control 8.23. For a clearer understanding, refer to ISO 27002, which provides more details about the Annex A controls. In Annex A of ISO 27001, control 8.23 is titled "Web Filtering" and states: "Access to external websites shall be managed to reduce exposure to malicious content." While it may seem, this control involves a WAF or similar web filtering mechanism, a deeper look into ISO 27002 reveals that this control focuses on enabling features on endpoints to mitigate the risks of personnel accessing websites with illegal content or those known to contain viruses or phishing material. Techniques to achieve this include blocking the IP address or domain of the concerned websites. Some browsers and anti-malware technologies perform this function automatically or can be configured to do so. Web filtering can employ a range of techniques, including signatures, heuristics, lists of acceptable or prohibited websites or domains, and bespoke configurations, all designed to prevent malicious software and other harmful activities from compromising the organization's network and systems. In general, if you have any doubts about a control, always refer to the detailed description and explanation in the ISO 27002 standard to get a crystal-clear understanding.

- It is a myth that penetration testing, whether for applications or networks, is an essential component of an ISO 27001 Information Security Management System (ISMS). This is one of the common misconceptions about ISO 27001. There is no specific requirement within the ISO clauses or ISO 27001 Annex A controls that mandates or addresses penetration testing. However, penetration tests can be very important for organizations to effectively manage security risks and protect against cyber-attacks, thereby supporting their vulnerability management program's objectives. Although ISO 27002 introduces penetration testing as one of the recommended methods for identifying technical vulnerabilities (see control 8.8 on page 92 of the ISO 27002:2022 standard), it is not a mandatory component of ISO

27001:2022 Annex A control 8.8. Additionally, penetration tests are recommended for the effectiveness of four other controls in ISO 27002:2022: control 5.21, control 8.16, control 8.25, and control 8.29.

- Control 5.11 of Annex A states: "Personnel and other interested parties, as appropriate, shall return all the organization's assets in their possession upon change or termination of their employment, contract, or agreement." While this control suggests that returning organizational assets is mandatory, it's important to understand that like any other control in Annex A, it may not be applicable in all cases. Many companies around the world choose not to require the return of laptops or other devices from employees after their employment ends for several reasons: 1. Cost of Return and Recycling: The return process, including shipping and handling, can be expensive. Additionally, recycling devices (reimaging, cleaning, and preparing them for new employees) can be more costly than purchasing new ones, 2. Encrypted Storage: Devices often have encrypted hard drives or internal storage, significantly reducing the risk of data leakage. This makes the actual risk of sensitive information being compromised very low.

Therefore, while the control uses the term "shall," implying a requirement, it is not necessarily mandatory in all situations. Organizations can assess their specific circumstances and determine whether this control is applicable. If deemed not applicable, this decision should be documented and justified based on the organization's risk management and security policies.

ISMS Audits

Audit Techniques

Information security audits are essential for evaluating the effectiveness and compliance of an organization's security controls and processes. Auditors typically employ four primary techniques: Inquiry, Observation, Inspection, and Reperformance. Each technique serves a specific purpose and provides unique insights into the organization's information security posture.

1. Inquiry

Inquiry involves talking to people within the organization to gather information and understand processes, policies, and controls.
This technique helps auditors gain insights into the organization's security culture, identify potential issues, and verify the understanding and implementation of security policies.
Examples:

- Conducting interviews with key personnel, such as IT managers, security officers, and compliance staff.
- Holding discussions with employees to understand their roles and responsibilities related to information security.
- Asking questions to clarify how specific security controls are implemented and maintained.

2. Observation

Observation involves watching processes and activities as they occur to assess how security controls are applied in practice.
This technique allows auditors to verify that processes are being followed as documented and to identify any deviations from established procedures.

Examples:

- Observing employees as they follow procedures for handling sensitive information.
- Watching how access control measures, such as biometric systems or badge readers, are used in real-time.
- Monitoring the process of incident response to see how effectively the organization handles security events.

3. Inspection

Inspection involves examining documentation, records, and system configurations to verify compliance with security policies and standards.
This technique helps auditors confirm that the necessary documentation exists, is up-to-date, and accurately reflects the organization's security practices.

Examples:

- Reviewing security policies, procedures, and guidelines.
- Examining system configurations, access logs, and audit trails.
- Inspecting records of security incidents, risk assessments, and vulnerability scans.

4. Reperformance

Reperformance involves the auditor independently executing a process to verify its accuracy and effectiveness.
This technique ensures that critical security processes are functioning correctly and that controls are effective in mitigating risks.

Examples:

- Reperforming a backup and restore process to verify data integrity and availability.
- Conducting a vulnerability scan to identify security weaknesses.
- Executing an access control procedure to confirm that only authorized individuals can access sensitive information.

Audit Stages

You might hear that the ISO 27001 audit consists of a stage 1 audit and a stage 2 audit. While this specific division isn't outlined in the ISO 27001 standard itself, it is detailed in ISO 27006. In practice, most auditors prefer conducting the audit in two stages: stage 1, which is primarily a tabletop audit or documentation review, and stage 2, which involves a system audit with extensive control testing. Though this two-stage process isn't explicitly required by ISO 27001, it is a common practice mentioned in ISO 27006.

Stage 1

According to ISO 27006, during the 1st stage of the audit, the certification body will obtain documentation on the design of the ISMS, covering the requirements specified in ISO 27001.
At a minimum, the client/auditee must provide the following information during stage 1 of the certification audit:

- General information concerning the ISMS and its activities.
- A copy of the required ISMS documentation specified in ISO/IEC 27001, along with any other necessary associated documentation.

The certification body will gain a thorough understanding of the ISMS design within the context of the client's organization, including risk assessment and treatment (such as determined controls), information security policies and objectives, and the client's overall preparedness for the audit. This understanding will inform the planning of the stage 2 audit.

The results of stage 1 must be documented in a written report. The certification body will review this report before deciding whether to proceed to stage 2. It will also confirm that the stage 2 audit team members possess the necessary competence, which may be validated by the auditor who led the stage 1 audit, if deemed appropriate.

ISO 27001 suggests involving a person from the certification body who was not part of the audit to review the report and confirm the competence of the stage 2 audit team as an additional layer of risk mitigation. However, other risk mitigation measures can also be implemented to achieve the same goal.

The certification body must inform the client about any additional types of information and records that may be required for detailed examination during stage 2.

Stage 2

Based on the findings from the stage 1 audit report, the certification body will develop an audit plan for stage 2. In addition to assessing the effective implementation of the ISMS, the main objective of stage 2 is to verify that the client *adheres to its own policies, objectives, and procedures*. This is a key part of lots of ISO standards.

This stage of the audit will focus on the following areas:

1. Top management leadership and commitment to the information security objectives.
2. Assessment of information security-related risks, ensuring that these assessments produce consistent, valid, and comparable results if repeated.
3. Determination of controls based on the information security risk assessment and risk treatment processes.
4. Evaluation of information security performance and the effectiveness of the ISMS against the information security objectives.
5. Correspondence between the determined controls, the

Statement of Applicability, the results of the information security risk assessment, the risk treatment process, and the information security policy and objectives.

6. Implementation of controls, taking into account the external and internal context and related risks, and the organization's monitoring, measurement, and analysis of information security processes and controls to determine if the declared controls are actually implemented and effective as a whole.

7. Examination of programs, processes, procedures, records, internal audits, and reviews of the ISMS effectiveness to ensure they are traceable to top management decisions and the information security policy and objectives.

Audit Findings in ISO 27001

In ISO 27001 audits, various types of findings can be identified, each indicating different levels of compliance issues or opportunities for improvement within the Information Security Management System (ISMS). The primary categories of audit findings are Opportunity for Improvement (OFI), Observation, Nonconformity, and Major Nonconformity.

1. Opportunity for Improvement (OFI)

- **Definition**: An OFI is a suggestion provided by the auditor to enhance the effectiveness or efficiency of the ISMS. It is not a mandatory requirement but a recommendation.
- **Impact**: Addressing OFIs can lead to better practices, improved processes, or greater efficiency within the ISMS.
- **Example**: The auditor might suggest more frequent internal training sessions to ensure staff are up to date with the latest security protocols.

2. Observation

- **Definition**: An observation is a comment made by the auditor regarding an aspect of the ISMS that could potentially lead to a nonconformity if not addressed. It indicates an area that, while not currently out of compliance, could benefit from attention.
- **Impact**: Observations are preventive and aim to alert the organization to potential future issues.
- **Example**: The auditor notes that documentation of a specific procedure is not as detailed as it could be, which might lead to misunderstandings or errors.

3. Nonconformity

- **Definition**: A nonconformity is a finding where the ISMS does not fully meet a requirement of the ISO 27001 standard or the organization's own documented procedures. It indicates a deviation from the specified requirements.
- **Impact**: Nonconformities require corrective actions to address the issue and ensure compliance with the standard.
- **Example**: The auditor discovers that risk assessments are not being conducted at the scheduled intervals defined in the ISMS policy.

4. Major Nonconformity

- **Definition**: A major nonconformity is a significant deviation from the ISO 27001 standard requirements, indicating a serious issue within the ISMS that affects its ability to achieve intended outcomes.
- **Impact**: Major nonconformities require immediate attention and substantial corrective actions. Failure to address major nonconformities can lead to suspension or withdrawal of the ISO 27001 certification.
- **Example**: The auditor finds that there is no evidence of management review meetings being conducted, which is a critical requirement of the ISMS.

Summary Table

Finding Type	Definition	Impact	Example
Opportunity for Improvement (OFI)	Suggestion to enhance ISMS effectiveness or efficiency	Not mandatory; can lead to better practices or greater efficiency	Suggesting more frequent internal training sessions
Observation	Comment on an aspect that could potentially lead to a nonconformity if not addressed	Preventive; alerts to potential future issues	Noting insufficient detail in procedure documentation
Nonconformity	Deviation from ISO 27001 requirements or organization's documented procedures	Requires corrective actions to ensure compliance	Risk assessments not conducted as scheduled
Major Nonconformity	Significant deviation affecting the ISMS's ability to achieve intended outcomes	Requires immediate and substantial corrective actions	Lack of evidence for management review meetings

Audit Types

ISO 27001 certification is typically valid for three years. However, to maintain the certification, organizations must undergo annual surveillance audits per ISO 27006. These audits ensure that the Information Security Management System (ISMS) continues to meet the ISO 27001 standard requirements and is effectively maintained.

Initial Certification Audit

Initial audit involves a review of the organization's ISMS documentation and operations to ensure it meets the ISO 27001 requirements and is effectively implemented and in operation. Initial ISO 27001 certification is issued for three years. However, it's important to remember that this certification has a limited duration. After being accredited, your certification will last for three years. By the time it expires, you should be more familiar with the renewal process.

Surveillance Audits

Surveillance audits are conducted annually over the three-year certification period and focus on ensuring that the ISMS is being maintained and continues to operate effectively. The auditor reviews any changes to the ISMS, the implementation of corrective actions, and the continual improvement process during surveillance audits.

Maintaining ISO 27001 certification through annual surveillance audits demonstrates the organization's commitment to continuous improvement and adherence to information security best practices.

Recertification Audit

Recertification audit is conducted before the three-year certification period expires. Similar to the initial certification audit, this audit reassesses the entire ISMS to ensure ongoing compliance with ISO 27001 so successful completion of the recertification audit extends the certification for another three-year cycle.

Special Audits

According to ISO 27006 and ISO 17021-1, there are special audits that can be used for various purposes. ISO 27001 special audits can be used to expand the scope, suspend, withdraw, or reduce the scope of certification. Another type of audit is the short-notice audit, where the certification body may conduct audits of a certified client at short notice or unannounced to investigate complaints, respond to changes, or follow up on a suspended client. However, these types of audits are not very common.

Correction vs Corrective Action

In the context of ISO 27001 audit, the terms "correction" and "corrective action" have distinct meanings and roles within the Information Security Management System (ISMS). Understanding the difference between these two terms is crucial for effective management and resolution of nonconformities.

Correction

- **Definition:** Correction is an action taken to eliminate a detected nonconformity. It addresses the immediate issue at hand.
- **Purpose:** The main aim of correction is to fix the problem quickly to restore compliance or proper functioning.
- **Scope:** Correction is typically a short-term fix and does not necessarily address the root cause of the nonconformity.
- **Example:** If an unauthorized user is found to have access to a secure area, the immediate correction might be to revoke the user's access rights.

Corrective Action

- **Definition:** Corrective action is a process aimed at eliminating the root cause of a detected nonconformity to prevent its recurrence.
- **Purpose:** The goal of corrective action is to address the underlying cause of the problem, ensuring that the issue does not happen again.
- **Scope:** Corrective actions are more comprehensive and long-term compared to corrections. They involve investigating the root cause, planning and implementing solutions, and monitoring their effectiveness.
- **Example:** In the case of unauthorized user access, the corrective action might involve reviewing and improving the access control policies and procedures to prevent such incidents in the future, training staff on these policies, and regularly auditing access controls.

Summary Table

Aspect	Correction	Corrective Action
Definition	Immediate action to fix a detected nonconformity	Process to eliminate the root cause of a nonconformity
Purpose	To restore compliance or proper functioning quickly	To prevent recurrence of the nonconformity
Scope	Short-term, addresses the symptom	Long-term, addresses the root cause

| Example | Revoking unauthorized access immediately | Revising access control policies and procedures |

Integrated Approach for Corrections & Corrective Actions

Implementing an integrated approach to identify and address issues within an Information Security Management System (ISMS) in accordance with ISO 27001 involves several key steps. This approach ensures that nonconformities are not only addressed immediately but also prevented from recurring by tackling their root causes. The steps include Detection, Correction, Investigation, Corrective Action, and Monitoring.

Detection: Identify the Nonconformity

- **Purpose**: To recognize and document any deviation from the ISMS requirements or the occurrence of security incidents.
- **Actions**:
    o Conduct regular internal audits and reviews.
    o Encourage reporting of incidents and nonconformities by staff.
    o Use automated monitoring tools to detect anomalies.
    o Record identified nonconformities in a centralized log for tracking.

Correction: Implement Immediate Fixes to Address the Issue

- **Purpose**: To take swift action to mitigate the impact of the nonconformity and restore normal operations of the ISMS.
- **Actions**:

- o   Implement immediate fixes to contain and correct the issue(s).
- o   Communicate the correction measures to relevant stakeholders.
- o   Document the actions taken to ensure traceability and accountability.

Investigation: Analyze the Root Cause of the Nonconformity

- **Purpose**: To understand the underlying reasons for the nonconformity and prevent future occurrences.
- **Actions**:
  - o   Conduct a thorough root cause analysis using techniques such as the 5 Whys or Fishbone Diagram.
  - o   Gather and analyze data from various sources, including audit reports, incident logs, and staff interviews.
  - o   Identify contributing factors and systemic issues that led to the nonconformity.

Corrective Action: Develop and Implement Measures to Eliminate the Root Cause

- **Purpose**: To develop and apply strategies that address the root cause and prevent recurrence.
- **Actions**:
  - o   Develop a corrective action plan that outlines specific steps to address the root cause.
  - o   Implement the corrective measures, which may include changes to policies, procedures, training programs, or technical controls.
  - o   Assign responsibilities and deadlines for the implementation of corrective actions.
  - o   Document the corrective actions and ensure they are approved by relevant management.

Monitoring: Ensure the Effectiveness of Corrective Actions and Prevent Recurrence

- **Purpose**: To verify that the corrective actions are effective and sustainable in the long term.
- **Actions**:
  - Monitor the implementation of corrective actions through follow-up audits and reviews.
  - Collect feedback from staff and stakeholders to assess the effectiveness of the measures.
  - Use performance indicators and metrics to measure improvements and identify any residual risks.
  - Update the risk assessment and ISMS documentation to reflect changes and lessons learned.
  - Ensure continuous improvement by incorporating findings into the organization's knowledge base and training programs.

Automated Implementation & Audits

Using automation solutions like Vanta, Secureframe, or Drata can significantly streamline the implementation and audit process for ISO 27001. These SaaS tools are designed to simplify the complexities involved in establishing and maintaining an Information Security Management System (ISMS), making the certification process more efficient and less resource intensive.

Benefits of Automation Solutions

1. **Streamlined Implementation**
   - **Automated Documentation**: These tools help automate the creation and management of essential documentation required for ISO 27001 compliance, such as policies,

procedures, and records.

- o **Pre-built Templates**: They offer pre-built templates and checklists that guide organizations through the implementation process, ensuring all necessary elements are covered.

2. **Integration with SaaS Providers**
   - o **Risk Management**: Integration with various SaaS providers enables continuous risk assessment and management by automatically pulling in data from cloud providers like AWS, Google Cloud, and Azure.
   - o **Continuous Monitoring**: These tools provide real-time monitoring of security controls, alerting organizations to potential issues and ensuring ongoing compliance with ISO 27001 requirements.

3. **Comprehensive Features**
   - o **Risk Register**: Tools like Vanta, Secureframe, and Drata include risk registers that help organizations identify, assess, and manage risks systematically.
   - o **Vendor/Supplier Management**: They offer modules for managing third-party vendors and suppliers, ensuring that they also comply with relevant security standards.
   - o **Security Awareness Programs**: These platforms can help implement and manage security awareness training programs for employees, ensuring that staff are knowledgeable about information security practices and policies.

4. **Efficiency in Audits**
   - o **Automated Evidence Collection**: These tools can automatically collect and organize evidence required for audits, reducing the manual effort involved in preparing for ISO 27001 audits.
   - o **Audit Readiness**: By maintaining continuous compliance and documentation, these

platforms help organizations stay audit-ready, minimizing the time and disruption caused by periodic audits.

Limitations and Considerations

1. **Lack of Advanced Security Tools**
   - **Vulnerability Scanners**: While these platforms offer a range of compliance and monitoring features, they typically do not include advanced security tools like vulnerability scanners. Organizations may still need to use separate tools to perform vulnerability assessments and scans.
   - **Comprehensive Security Suite**: For a complete security solution, additional tools may be required to cover areas such as endpoint protection, intrusion detection systems, and advanced threat protection.
2. **Customization and Flexibility**
   - **Tailored Solutions**: Although these platforms provide a lot of built-in functionality, they might not cater to all specific needs or unique scenarios of every organization. Customization might be limited compared to in-house solutions.
   - **Dependence on SaaS Providers**: Relying on third-party SaaS providers means that any changes or updates to the platform are controlled by the provider, which may affect how certain features are used or integrated.

Accreditation Bodies

A common question about ISO 27001 certification is whether the certification body must be a member of the International Accreditation Service (IAS) or other accreditation bodies. The answer is no. However, accreditation bodies play a crucial role in ensuring the competence and reliability of certification bodies. They independently verify if a conformity assessment body meets specific criteria and is competent to perform assessment tasks, including testing, calibration, inspection, and certification of management systems, products, and services.

Accreditation bodies typically derive their authority from governments and validate the capabilities of certification bodies according to standards such as ISO/IEC 17011. While most countries have a single accreditation authority, the United States has multiple, such as IAS and ANAB. IAS accredited certification programs for individuals, products, and management systems according to standards like ISO/IEC 17024, ISO/IEC 17065, and ISO/IEC 17021-1. ANAB supervises certification bodies accredited against ISO/IEC 17021-1.

Furthermore, international groups like the European co-operation for Accreditation (EA) and the International Accreditation Forum (IAF) work towards certifying competent organizations and establishing mutual recognition agreements among their members. This cooperation helps ensure that accreditation bodies maintain high standards of competence and reliability globally.

Personal Certifications

Obtaining personal certificates related to ISO 27001 and ISO 27701 demonstrates an individual's expertise and competence in implementing and auditing information security management systems (ISMS) and privacy information management systems (PIMS). These certifications are highly valued in the information security and data privacy fields.

ISO 27001 Lead Implementer

This certification is designed for professionals responsible for implementing and managing an ISMS based on ISO 27001. This certification validates expertise in ISMS implementation, enhances career opportunities in information security management, and helps organizations achieve and maintain ISO 27001 certification. Different issuers cover different topics but most of them cover the following areas in their training and exams:

- Planning and initiating the implementation of an ISMS.
- Implementing and managing ISMS policies, controls, and procedures.
- Monitoring, measuring, and improving the ISMS.

ISO 27001 Lead Auditor

This certification is intended for professionals who audit ISMS for conformance with ISO 27001. This certification demonstrates competence in auditing ISMS, qualifies individuals to lead ISO 27001 audits, and supports organizations in maintaining compliance with ISO 27001. Different issuers cover different topics but most of them cover the following areas in their training and exams:

- Planning and conducting ISO 27001 audits.
- Managing an audit program.
- Reporting audit findings and follow-up.

Benefits of Personal Certifications

- **Professional Recognition**: Certifications are globally recognized and enhance the credibility of professionals in the field of information security and data privacy.
- **Career Advancement**: Certified professionals are often preferred by employers and can command higher salaries.
- **Organizational Compliance**: Certified professionals help organizations achieve and maintain compliance with international standards, improving overall security and privacy posture.
- **Knowledge and Skills**: Certification programs provide in-depth knowledge and practical skills required for implementing and auditing ISMS and PIMS.

Certification Process

1. **Training**: Attend an accredited training course for the specific certification.
2. **Examination**: Pass the certification exam, which tests knowledge and skills related to the standard and its implementation or auditing.
3. **Experience**: Some certifications require a certain level of professional experience in information security or privacy management.
4. **Application**: Submit an application to the certification body, providing evidence of training, exam results, and relevant experience.

Maintaining Certification

- **Continual Professional Development (CPD)**: Engage in ongoing learning and professional development activities to stay current with industry trends and best practices.
- **Recertification**: Some certifications require periodic

recertification to ensure continued competence and adherence to evolving standards.

ISO 27001 vs NIST CSF

ISO 27001 is a certifiable risk centric and document-driven international framework with an emphasis on a structured and continuous improvement approach to information security while NIST CSF is very outcome-focused and more flexible than ISO 27001. Both frameworks have their unique advantages, and organizations may choose to implement one or both depending on their specific requirements, regulatory environment, and strategic objectives.

NIST CSF

The NIST Cybersecurity Framework (CSF) is a voluntary framework developed by the National Institute of Standards and Technology (NIST) to provide a policy framework of computer security guidance for how private sector organizations in the United States can assess and improve their ability to prevent, detect, and respond to cyber attacks. The framework is designed to help organizations better understand, manage, and reduce their cybersecurity risks and protect their networks and data. Its structure is totally different from the structure of ISO 27001.

The NIST CSF is structured around three main components: Core, Tiers, and Profiles.

Core

The latest version of NIST CSF consists of six functions: Govern, Identify, Protect, Detect, Respond, and Recover.

Profiles

A CSF Organizational Profile outlines an organization's current and/or desired cybersecurity posture based on the Core's outcomes. It helps tailor, assess, prioritize, and communicate cybersecurity efforts considering mission objectives, stakeholder expectations, threat landscape, and requirements. This ensures prioritized actions and effective communication with stakeholders. Each profile includes Current Profile:

Describes the outcomes an organization is currently achieving and the extent of these achievements. Target Profile: Defines desired outcomes prioritized for future cybersecurity risk management, considering anticipated changes such as new requirements, technology, and threat trends. You can download a very good profile template from https://www.nist.gov/profiles-0 and start your NIST CSF journey.

Implementation Tiers

Helps organizations understand the degree to which their cybersecurity practices are robust and implemented. We also call it "Maturity Level" in the cybersecurity world. An organization can use the Tiers to inform its Current and Target Profiles. Tiers characterize the rigor of an organization's cybersecurity risk governance and management practices, providing context for its approach to cybersecurity risks. The Tiers range from Partial (Tier 1), Risk Informed (Tier 2), Repeatable (Tier 3), to Adaptive (Tier 4), describing a progression from informal, ad hoc responses to agile, risk-informed, and continuously improving approaches. Selecting Tiers helps set the overall tone for managing cybersecurity risks.

Although NIST CSF was originally designed for use in US federal sectors, it is flexible and adaptable to different industries and sectors, allowing organizations to prioritize activities and allocate resources effectively.

ISO 27001 Philosophy

- **Risk Management-Centric:** ISO 27001 is fundamentally built around a risk management approach. It focuses on identifying, evaluating, and treating information security risks through a structured Information Security Management System (ISMS).
- **Prescriptive and Certifiable:** ISO 27001 provides specific requirements and controls that organizations must implement to achieve certification. It prescribes a

set of practices that need to be in place.

- **Continuous Improvement:** Unlike many other information security frameworks, ISO 27001 encourages continuous improvement of the information security program.
- **International Standard:** As an international standard, ISO 27001 aims to provide a universally accepted framework for managing information security, applicable across different industries and countries.

NIST CSF Philosophy

- **Framework-Based and Flexible:** NIST CSF is designed as a voluntary framework that provides a set of guidelines, best practices, and standards for improving cybersecurity risk management. It is more flexible and adaptable to different organizational contexts.
- **Outcome-Focused:** NIST CSF emphasizes outcomes rather than prescriptive controls. It focuses on the functions of identify, protect, detect, respond, and recover.
- **Tailorable to Needs:** NIST CSF is designed to be tailored to the specific needs, risk tolerances, and threat landscapes of different organizations, particularly within the United States.
- **Sector-Specific Guidance:** NIST CSF includes sector-specific guidance, which allows it to be highly relevant to various industries.

About the Authors

Ben Pournader (CGEIT, CDPSE, CISM, CISA, CRISC) is a Senior Information Security Program Manager with a distinguished career, having worked for prominent companies in Silicon Valley, including Facebook, LinkedIn, and Cisco. With nearly 25 years of experience in IT and security, Ben has a deep expertise in Information Security Engineering and Cybersecurity Management.

Throughout his career, Ben has played a pivotal role in helping numerous organizations build and enhance their cybersecurity programs and Information Security Management Systems.

Ben is a one-man army who is not only good at cybersecurity operations, information security and cloud architecture but also a subject matter expert in information security and privacy compliance inducing PCI DSS, ISO 27001, ISO 27002, ISO 27017, ISO 27018, ISO 27701, ISO 22301, HIPAA, HITRUST, GDPR, CCPA, GLBA, FedRAMP, CMMC, SOC 2, SOX, NYDFS Cybersecurity Regulation (NYCRR 500), FFIEC, NIST standards (NIST Cybersecurity Framework, NIST 800-30, NIST 800-53, NIST 800-63, NIST 800-171, ...) and so on.

A cancer survivor, Ben began writing this book and three others in 2018, but his treatment delayed their completion. Now, cancer-free, he has returned to finishing his writing projects, starting with "Ben's Pocket Guide to PCI DSS 3.2.1," which he completed in 2020.

Behzad Saei is an experienced professional in the field of Information Security Management, specializing in consulting, implementing, and auditing ISO 27001. With five years of hands-on experience, Behzad has successfully guided numerous organizations through the complexities of achieving and maintaining ISO 27001 certification. His deep understanding of the standard, combined with practical insights from real-world implementations, makes him a trusted expert in the field. Behzad's dedication to strengthening information security frameworks has earned him recognition as a reliable consultant and auditor in the industry.

Made in the USA
Columbia, SC
25 September 2024